Measuring Human Abilities

Philip Merrifield, *Editor*

NEW DIRECTIONS FOR TESTING AND MEASUREMENT
WILLIAM B. SCHRADER, *Editor-in-Chief*

Number 12, December 1981

Paperback sourcebooks in
The Jossey-Bass Social and Behavioral Sciences Series

Jossey-Bass Inc., Publishers
San Francisco • Washington • London

Measuring Human Abilities
Number 12, December 1981
   Philip Merrifield, *Editor*

New Directions for Testing and Measurement Series
William B. Schrader, *Editor-in-Chief*

New Directions for Testing and Measurement is published
quarterly by Jossey-Bass Inc., Publishers. Subscriptions, single-issue
orders, change of address notices, undelivered copies, and other
correspondence should be sent to *New Directions* Subscriptions,
Jossey-Bass Inc., Publishers, 433 California Street, San Francisco,
California 94104.

Editorial correspondence should be sent to the Editor-in-Chief,
William B. Schrader, ETS, Princeton, New Jersey 08541.

Library of Congress Catalogue Card Number LC 80-85265
International Standard Serial Number ISSN 0271-0609
International Standard Book Number ISBN 87589-874-2

Cover art by Willi Baum
Manufactured in the United States of America

Ordering Information

The paperback sourcebooks listed below are published quarterly and can be ordered either by subscription or as single copies.

Subscriptions cost $30.00 per year for institutions, agencies, and libraries. Individuals can subscribe at the special rate of $18.00 per year *if payment is by personal check.* (Note that the full rate of $30.00 applies if payment is by institutional check, even if the subscription is designated for an individual.) Standing orders are accepted.

Single copies are available at $6.95 when payment accompanies order, and *all single-copy orders under $25.00 must include payment.* (California, Washington, D.C., New Jersey, and New York residents please include appropriate sales tax.) For billed orders, cost per copy is $6.95 plus postage and handling. (Prices subject to change without notice.)

To ensure correct and prompt delivery, all orders must give either the *name of an individual* or an *official purchase order number.* Please submit your order as follows:

Subscriptions: specify series and subscription year.
Single Copies: specify sourcebook code and issue number (such as, TM8).

Mail orders for United States and Possessions, Latin America, Canada, Japan, Australia, and New Zealand to:
    Jossey-Bass Inc., Publishers
    433 California Street
    San Francisco, California 94104

Mail orders for all other parts of the world to:
    Jossey-Bass Limited
    28 Banner Street
    London EC1Y 8QE

New Directions for Testing and Measurement Series
William B. Schrader, *Editor-in-Chief*

Contents

Editor's Notes

The plans of editors, like those of others, often go astray. When this volume was first proposed, a much greater emphasis on techniques of measurement was envisioned than has turned out to be the case. I believe, however, that the issues of goals and restrictions addressed here are current and are logically prior to consideration of new instrumentation. For the discrepancies that remain, I offer my deep apologies.

One of the restrictions that must be considered in the development of aptitude tests is the avoidance of bias. Scheuneman addresses these issues at the item level, with special attention to the role of external criteria. Her new model of item bias specifies the degree to which the ability of an individual may be underestimated, particularly as a function of the distance from novel item formats and unusual methods or strategies to his own life experiences. The implication is that clear instructions and examples are necessary to avoid bias. It is not clear what should be done to avoid bias when the aptitude to be measured is heavily involved with strategy of problem analysis, that is, deciding what the problem really is or transforming one description to another.

Hennessy highlights the problems of using traditional measures, such as IQ, which seem to work against the goals of differential diagnosis, placement, and remediation of children with learning disabilities. In this domain, characteristically the child is deficient in only a few of the many aptitudes, or developed skills, that contribute to school achievement. He reviews several recent developments as sources of new approaches to the multiple and differential assessment of children's aptitudes.

Hummel-Rossi presents a detailed analysis of a longitudinal study of aptitudes as predictors of school achievement. After showing the validity of figural analogies and verbal classification tasks for eighth-grade performance, she investigates the effect of how teachers treat their students, as measured by a simple teacher self-report regarding each student. It is clear that teachers engage differently with students who differ in aptitudes and to some extent in personality traits. The effects of differentiated treatment by eighth-grade teachers persist in tenth-grade performance when different teachers are giving grades. Patterns of regressions of performance on aptitudes differ for different student groups defined by the treatment variables. In general, differences in personality traits and sex made little difference in the relations of performance to aptitudes. In this sample, ethnic differences and socioeconomic differences were small, so bias was not investigated.

With regard to my own presentation, suffice it to say that although the TETRA model may be seen as derivative, it differs in important ways from Guilford's SOI model. Transforming is seen as a process of thought, not as a product; the unfortunate contrast between divergent and convergent thinking that makes them appear as opposites is recast to show how they are related positively to each other; self is introduced as one of four things that it is basic to think about (the other three are forms, ideas, and other persons); and the dimension of product is reconceptualized as a matter of the thinker's attention to a self-defined level of complexity, making it a personalistic rather than a task-determined aspect of thought. In general, each of the SOI categories can be defined in terms of the new model, and the higher-level intellectual behaviors such as problem-solving can be described. Guilford's recent statement regarding orthogonality of factors is discussed. Implications of the TETRA model for new measures of aptitude are developed.

We had intended to include a chapter on latent-trait analysis, because of its currency and relevance to the problems of aptitude measurement. Unfortunately, our author, for various good reasons, was unable to meet his commitment, and by then it was too late to arrange for another contributor. From my own point of view, then, I shall presume to comment on one recent development, a welcome event in view of the almost twenty years of applications to item calibration with little attention to the aptitude portion of the Rasch model. Whitely (1981, see reference in my chapter) has put together what she calls a multicomponent model by applying the one-parameter logistic model to each of three components in turn. I am concerned not only that this does not address the problem of multiple concurrent aptitudes, as is the case in traditional factor or regression approaches, but that she assumes the components to be independent when, by her definition, they are sequentially dependent. The intercorrelations among these component scores are artificially high in one case and low in another; when these correlations are introduced into a structural equation analysis for weights, the interpretation of the results must be ambiguous at best. Although there are several sources of confusion in the article cited, stemming from editorial oversights for the most part, I would applaud the effort to quantify the relation between a person's ability level and an item. One should remember that factor abilities at the individual level are obtained as factor scores, and that in Thurstone's accounting equation, the test scores are weighted composites of the factor scores; how this model differs in essence from one in which the test score is regressed on component scores escapes me. A test, however labelled, is not a factor. My recollections of extensive discussions during the item-writing stages of test development under Guilford's guidance leads me to empathize with Moliere's protagonist: perhaps we were doing component analysis and didn't know it! Or perhaps it is another example of the importance of documenting the how as well as the what of one's research. In any case, a closer inspection of the many items for many factors developed in that situation might be fruitful for further work in latent-trait analysis.

Philip Merrifield
Editor

*Item bias is reconceptualized to include disance of item content
from respondent's experience, and the effects of differing
values of mean and standard deviation for bias parameter are
explored in a simulation.*

A New Look at Bias
in Aptitude Tests

Janice Dowd Scheuneman

The topic of bias in tests and test items has appeared often in the measurement literature since the late 1960s, when interest in the subject was stimulated by the civil rights activism of that period. Despite this continued interest, however, relatively little progress has been made in understanding how bias operates in tests or what the sources of bias are, and there has been even less progress in devising ways of reducing the impact of bias on scores. The general lack of progress or even of clear-cut results has led many researchers to conclude that there is little if any bias in tests and that what bias there is contributes little to the observed group differences in test scores.

The question of bias arises from observed differences between the performance of various groups—whether these groups are defined by social class, ethnic backround, or sex. Particularly in the case of aptitude tests, minority group spokespersons and other critics of testing have claimed that group differences in performance must be exclusively the result of bias in tests. Others, however, would agree with Green (1978, p. 13), who stated, "Tests of general verbal and numerical skills are usually called aptitude tests, which is unfortunate since the term *aptitude* seems to suggest an inborn, unchangeable trait. Actually, the tests assess developed abilities—skills acquired through years of training and practice with verbal and numerical material. Aptitudes do not develop without nurturing. Education is necessary." This view expresses the position of those who say that tests are only the messengers who bring bad

P. Merrifield (Ed.). *New Directions for Testing and Measurement: Measuring Human Abilities*, no. 12.
San Francisco: Jossey-Bass, December 1981.

news of the effects of educational and economic inequities in American society. The effects of discrimination are undeniable, so this argument is compelling to most measurement specialists and other educational researchers. Even if this assertion is true, however, it is still possible that bias is also operating to inflate observed score differences, and in no way does it absolve us as researchers from examining our tests and attempting to assess the extent of our own contribution to performance differences that result from the way in which we build tests.

Bias is a complex concept that means different things to the critics and defenders of testing. In research on the subject, bias has typically been defined in operational terms. Such definitions generally fall into two broad categories. The first category of definitions most often involves the whole test or test score and an external criterion against which the test performance can be evaluated. The second group of definitions emphasizes the relations among test items and their relation to the total test, and it rarely involves external criteria.

The total test or criterion definitions arose primarily from concern about bias in tests used for selection. This kind of bias is often referred to as *bias in selection* or *test fairness*. This group of definitions can again be divided into two major classes, which might be characterized as differential validity approaches and regression approaches. The differential validity approaches seek correlation coefficients between the test score and the criterion measure. Bias is presumed to exist if a test is valid for one but not the other of two groups being compared. This is sometimes referred to as single-group validity. Alternatively, the correlations for both groups may be greater than zero but significantly different from each other (Humphreys, 1973).

The regression approach defines bias in terms of differences in the regression of the criterion measure on the test score. The most commonly cited definition is that of Cleary (1968, p. 115): "A test is biased for members of a subgroup of the population if, in the prediction of a criterion for which the test was designed, consistent nonzero errors of prediction are made for members of the subgroup. In other words, the test is biased if the criterion score predicted from the common regression line is consistently too high or too low for members of the subgroup. With this definition of bias, there may be a connotation of 'unfair,' particularly if the use of the test produces a prediction that is too low."

Although this definition appears to be reasonable, other researchers, particularly Thorndike (1971a) and Darlington (1971), have pointed out that other reasonable definitions using a regression model lead to mutually contradictory results except in those few cases where the predictor is perfectly valid or the criterion measure is perfectly unbiased. That is, in most cases, an item that is unbiased under the Cleary definition would be biased under one of the other definitions and vice versa. In addition to pointing out a number of logical anomalies that result from the use of Cleary's definition, Darlington notes that, when a test is unbiased by this definition, "then the test is affected directly by culture, capitalizing on the correlation between culture and criterion in order to maximize validity" (1971, p. 77). Darlington defines the culturally fair test in these terms: "Although for predictive purposes we think of X as an independent variable and Y as a dependent variable, thinking in causal terms suggests a reversal of this relation. We consider the criterion Y to be an ability (to succeed in school, say). A subject's score on test X is influenced both by this ability and by the subject's cultural background [C] . . . . Suppose we define test X as culturally fair only if C has no direct effect on X, independent of Y. In other words, this definition requires that C and X must be uncorrelated in a subset of people with the same Y scores" (1971, p. 75). This definition may be stated another way by saying that, on the average, people in different groups with the same criterion score will have the same test score.* Darlington concludes that "If a conflict arises between the two goals of maximizing a test's validity and minimizing the test's discrimination against certain cultural groups, then a subjective policy-level decision must be made concerning the relative importance of the two goals" (1971, p. 71).

The conflict between selection goals led to the elaboration of a new set of models, based on decision theory, through which the utility of certain outcomes could be specified and the results of various decision rules could be evaluated. These models have all been reviewed elsewhere (for example, Jensen, 1980, or Petersen and Novick, 1976), and they are more properly described as models of bias not in the test but in the selection rule. Since the focus of this chapter is on bias in tests, these decision theoretic approaches will not be discussed here.

While the furor raged over models of bias in selection, another approach to the study of bias was being explored. In this approach, no external criteria of performance were used. While a number of operational definitions were proposed, most could be summarized as stating that unbiased items should function in the same way for two subgroups of the test population. These definitions and their related statistical models and indices have come to be referred to as *item bias techniques*.

Most definitions of item bias can be subsumed under one or the other of two general headings: definitions related to an item-by-group interaction concept and definitions that are conditional on ability. The item-by-group interaction approach was first used by Cardall and Coffman (1964). Using this conceptualization, Cleary and Hilton (1968, p. 61) defined bias as follows: "An item of a test is considered biased for members of a particular group if the

---

*It is interesting to note that Jensen (1980) rejects Darlington's definition by pointing out, as Darlington did, that the Cleary and Darlington definitions are incompatible. Having earlier used Cleary's formulation to define an unbiased test, he states: "this [Darlington's] rule runs into serious difficulty, for it contradicts our core definition of an unbiased test except in the unrealistic limiting case where the test has *perfect* validity . . . . In other words, only a *biased* test (or other biased predictor) can possibly satisfy the condition [set by this rule]" (Jensen, 1980, p. 396).

item produces an uncommon discrepancy between the performance of that group and the performance of other groups. That is, the members of the group obtain an average score which differs from the average score of other groups by more or less than expected from their performance on other items of the same test." Basically, this definition suggests that the real differences in performance between two groups on individual test items can be accounted for by the group main effect in an analysis of variance (ANOVA) context and bias by the item-by-group interaction. Results from ANOVAs have not often been reported in the literature on item bias, however. The so-called transformed item difficulty approaches, which are conceptually related, have been applied far more often. In these techniques, the item difficulty values (percent of correct responses) are transformed in order to make the relationship between difficulty values for two groups more nearly linear. Again, it is assumed that the difficulty values of unbiased items should be uniformly related for two groups that differ in ability (Angoff, in press; Angoff and Ford, 1973).

The second major type of definition is conditional on ability. My own definition (Scheuneman, 1975, 1979) is analogous to that suggested by Darlington (1971) in the predictive bias case. In that case, "An unbiased item is defined as an item for which the probability of a correct response is the same for all persons of a given ability, regardless of their ethnic group membership" (Scheuneman, 1979, p. 145). This conception of bias is shared by a whole family of procedures. In some, raw score has provided a measure of ability; in others, estimated true score (Lord, 1977; Rudner, 1977). Descriptions and discussion of the different statistical models and methodologies of item bias have been provided by Rudner, Getson, and Knight (1980a).

All these conceptualizations of bias depend to a greater or lesser extent on operational definitions that specify how bias can be detected if it is present in a test. Unfortunately, these definitions were developed without a clearly articulated theory of bias and how it operates to affect scores. This is hardly unusual, however, in a new field of inquiry. Flaugher (1978, p. 678) describes the problem that arises from such lack of theory when he warns, "We continually run the risk of losing perspective on our research when we settle on one operational definition of test bias as a scientific starting point and then proceed to forget that it is only that." Shepard (in press) likewise notes the appealing simplicity of operational definitions that fail to embrace the complexity of the bias issue.

In this chapter, my major thesis is that aptitude tests are essentially valid for minority groups but that they are also "biased" in the sense that they underestimate the true ability of minority group examinees. In this conceptualization of bias, I see validity of the test scores, as it is usually evaluated, as a necessary but not a sufficient condition for an unbiased test. Petersen (1980, p. 103) reminds us that "bias is a statistical term. It means that the expected error of estimate is not zero. To say that a measurement device is biased is to say that the average observation is not equal to the 'true' value." This view of bias was stated in another way by Schmidt and Hunter (1974, p. 2): "Tests equally valid for blacks and whites are equally successful in properly rank ordering individuals *within* both races on future criterion performance; however, they may be unfairly biased in that they place one race *as a group* too high or too low relative to the other." Notice that bias is thus defined in reference to the "true" status of the unobservable or latent ability that is presumed to be measured by the test. Hence, the evidence for the existence of bias defined in this way, without an intervening operational definition, must be indirect.

In the next section of this chapter, I will evaluate the evidence provided by studies of test and item bias as it relates to this thesis. In the final section, I will outline a theory of bias that is broader in scope and more precisely formulated than previous conceptualizations. I will then show how this conceptualization relates to other areas of research and how it permits us to explain results previously unnoted or thought to be anomalous if tests are biased as more narrowly defined. I will restrict my discussion primarily to studies involving aptitude tests used in educational, as opposed to industrial or military, settings and to bias related to blacks. This will serve only to simplify the argument, not to suggest that bias does not exist for other types of tests, for other minority groups, or in other settings. The hypothesis that aptitude tests are unbiased has sought much of its support from the absence of plausible alternative explanations of the evidence. The purpose of this chapter is to provide an alternative.

Evidence for Bias

The literature on bias can be divided into three broad areas: works that deal with the whole test and use external criteria to evaluate possible bias; works that deal with the whole test and do not use external criteria, such as studies of factor structure and patterns of item difficulty; and works dealing with specific test items, most of which do not use external criteria. Members of the third group have been identified as *item bias* studies. In his discussion of bias in aptitude tests, Jensen (1980) deals primarily with the first two types of studies, which he refers to as *predictive validity* studies and *construct validity* studies, respectively. Although he describes some of the methodology for item bias as part of the construct validity approach, he does not review the results of item bias studies. My review of the first two areas draws heavily on his compilation.

In my review of this literature, I will seek evidence that the tests are fundamentally valid but that bias exists in the form of underestimation of ability for minority group persons. This evidence will derive primarily from the predictive validity and construct validity studies. I will also seek evidence for process differences in responding to items that may account, in part, for such underestimates. If process differences exist, they will be demonstrated by studies of factor structure and by studies of internal relationships among the items of a test. I will stay as far away from the issue of fairness as I can, although it will be necessary to discuss it under predictive bias. In that discussion, I will try to maintain Jensen's distinction between bias and fairness. "The assessment of bias," he states, " is a purely objective, empirical, statistical, and quantitative matter entirely independent of subjective value judgments and ethical issues concerning fairness or unfairness of tests and the uses to which they are put (Jensen, 1980, p. 375).

Predictive Validity Studies

One approach to bias in prediction is the regression approach. To repeat a point made earlier, Cleary (1968) states that the regression planes for two groups will be equal for an unbiased test. This means that the standard error of estimate, the slope, and the intercept will be equal for the two groups. Let us set aside the objections to this definition for the moment and examine the research findings.

Linn (1973) reviewed three studies using scores on the Scholastic Aptitude Test (SAT) to predict freshman grade point averages (Cleary, 1968; Davis and Kerner-Hoeg, 1971; Temp, 1971). Of the twenty-two cases reported in these studies, only eight showed equality of regression on all three statistics.* In predictions of Metropolitan Achievement Test scores in reading and math from the Wechsler Intelligence Scale for Children, Revised (WISC-R) in grades 1, 3, 5, 7, and 9, Reschly and Sabers (1979) report that only five of the ten regression planes have equal regressions, despite the very small samples, where power could be expected to be low. Jensen (1980, pp. 475–476) reports a study by Farr and others (1971) in which the California Tests of Mental Maturity were used to predict course grades, overall grade point average, class rank, and ratings of leadership and creativity in grades 9 and 12. Of the fifteen regressions reported, only six, four at grade 9 and two at grade 12, had equal regressions on all three statistics. Jensen (1980, pp. 487–488) also reports a study by Centra, Linn, and Parry (1970) and one by Farr and others (1971) that predicted freshman college grades from SAT scores. In both studies, four out of five predictions show equal regressions. Studies by Pfeifer and Sedlacek (1971) and Goldman and Hewitt (1976), which also used SAT scores to predict freshman college grades, found that only two regressions out of seven were equal for black and white students.

To summarize: In fifty-nine reported regression comparisons, regression planes were equal on all three statistics — standard error of estimate, slope, and intercept — in twenty-five. This amounts to about 42 percent of the cases in which the tests appeared to be unbiased and 58 percent of the cases in which the tests appeared to be biased. In the thirty-four cases in which the

---

*In fact, the differences in the standard error of estimate were not tested in Cleary's study, so that five of the eight cases had no difference on only two of the statistics.

hypothesis was rejected, there were differences in the error of estimate in four-teen, differences in slope in eight, and differences in intercept in eleven. In one case, differences were not tested, since validity coefficients for both groups were essentially zero.

The results of studies in which bias is defined by unequal regression planes are dismissed in most instances, however, because tests so biased appear not to result in "unfair" selection. Cleary notes that "with this definition, there may be a connotation of 'unfair,' particularly if the use of the test produces a prediction that is too low" (Cleary, 1968, p. 115). In the studies just cited, however, when the regression planes are not equal, the effect typically has been an overprediction of the criterion. That is, the criterion scores obtained by the black students are generally lower than the criterion scores predicted for them. Hence, the reasoning goes, these tests are not unfair.

For instance, despite Jensen's call for a distinction between bias and fairness, he concludes his review of predictive bias studies with this statement: "In the vast majority of studies, the regressions of criterion performance on test scores do not differ for blacks and whites. And almost without exception, when the white and black regressions do differ significantly, the difference is in the intercepts, with the black intercept below the white.* This intercept bias results in overprediction of the blacks' criterion performance when predictions for whites and blacks are based on the white or on the common regression line . . . . Thus, contrary to popular belief, the evidence shows that, when predic-tive test bias is found, it in fact most often favors blacks in any selection proce-dure that treats all test scores alike regardless of race . . . . It seems safe to conclude that most standard ability and aptitude tests in current use in educa-tion . . . are not biased for blacks or whites with respect to criterion validity" (Jensen, 1980, p. 515).

This conclusion—that the tests may be biased but that they are also fair, since they actually favor blacks—has been challenged on a number of grounds. Thorndike (1971a) pointed out that even if criterion scores are over-predicted, the resulting procedure typically selects fewer blacks than justified by their ability to succeed on the criterion. By examining the records of enrolled students, Goldman and Widawski (1976) were able to evaluate the impact of various admissions criteria on selection errors. They found that the addition of SAT scores to high school grade point averages improved prediction slightly, but that the kinds of error changed. Addition of SAT scores resulted in a de-

---

*The studies cited here do not exactly duplicate those cited by Jensen. I included all studies using school or college settings for which regressions were provided by Jen-sen, and I supplemented these with one or two others. In some cases, I used the original paper to obtain more detail than Jensen provided. He also included several studies of test use in the military and in job settings that I did not examine. However, my tabula-tion suggests that to say that a "vast majority" shows no regression bias may be an over-statement. Moreover, findings that regression differences occurred only in intercepts were hardly without exception, even in this subset of studies.

crease in false positive errors (accepting students who will fail) and an increase in false negative errors (rejecting students who will pass). Swinton (1981) points out that, if the students in a study have been preselected by something like a cutting score on the predictor (this is apt to be true in studies of college admissions) and if two groups differ in predictor mean score prior to selection (as they will if all students are included), overprediction will result from simple regression of criterion scores toward the appropriate within-group means, and this overprediction will increase as the original cutting rule becomes more stringent. Using a formulation of bias like Darlington's (1971), Weitzman (1979) demonstrated that maximization of predictive validity through use of a regression model has the effect of maximizing the correlation between race and predictor score for a given value of the criterion. He shows also that there is very little reduction in validity if the prediction is adjusted to minimize the correlation between race and predictor for given criterion scores. None of these objections to the Cleary definition appears to support the conclusion that fairness results from the use of tests unbiased by this rule.

In view both of such criticism and of the flaws noted by Darlington (1971), continued use of the Cleary formulation for the study of bias in prediction is remarkable. Indeed, the Cleary formulation is by far the one most often adopted for studies of predictive bias. Whatever the failings of this approach, however, if we look only at the statistical results cited here, the 58 percent of cases in which the regressions are unequal strongly suggests that bias is more than a chance or random occurrence. If the regression planes are not equal, one possible explanation is that the test scores are not unbiased estimates of ability for black examinees.

A second approach to the study of bias in prediction looks at differential validity. In this approach, bias is defined as the result of unequal correlations (predictive validity coefficients) between the predictor and the criterion for two or more groups of interest. This approach is common in the literature on the use of tests for job selection. This literature has been reviewed by Boehm (1972), Fincher (1975), and Jensen (1980). In general, the results appear to indicate that differential validity does not often occur, although Katzell and Dyer (1977) have argued that the evidence provided so far is inadequate, so the case for the importance of differential validity should not be dismissed too quickly.

Differential validity has not been treated explicitly in the literature on educational measurement. The correlations between predictor and criterion are usually reported, however. I have reviewed the studies reported by Jensen (1980), together with others that reported such correlations. In the fifteen studies tabulated,* fifty-three correlation comparisons were possible. Of these,

*The studies tabulated here are Stanley and Porter (1967), two correlation comparisons; Hills (1964), one comparison; Thorndike (1971b), six comparisons; Crano, Kenny, and Campbell (1972), one comparison; Green and Farquhar (1965), two com-

twenty-five were higher for whites, twenty-three were higher for blacks, and four were the same. This comparison did not take differences in sample size, type of test, criterion measure, or age level into account, and it cannot be taken as evidence against differential validity. Nonetheless, no pattern suggesting that the tests as a whole are more valid or less valid for blacks is evident.

One explanation of the equivocal nature of the results on differential validity lies in the nature of the comparison of correlation coefficients, particularly when these are based on samples of different size. Swinton (1981) provides a good discussion of the problems encountered. Other problems are illustrated by Pine and Weiss (1976). In that study, they simulated test performance using Birnbaum's three-parameter latent trait formulation* to establish the probability of correct response to items of varying difficulty for two hypothetical groups whose members were equal in underlying ability. Bias was systematically added by reducing the probability of a correct response for one group. To do this, the difficulty parameter of all items was altered by equivalent amounts in each hypothetical test. Because these were simulated data, the elusive criterion of a perfectly valid and unbiased measure of true ability was available here. To the extent that true ability is at least in part a function of educational opportunity, which means that it is unlikely to be equal for the members of both groups, and to the extent that real-world criteria are far from perfect, the results were not as realistic as we could wish. This study clearly demonstrated, however, that the correlation of test scores with true ability varied not only with the degree of bias introduced but as a complex function of item discrimination, test length, and the distribution of item difficulties (peaked versus rectangular distributions). These psychometric characteristics of tests have received little attention in examinations of the effects of test properties on ethnic-group performance.

I believe that the case for the existence of substantial differential valid-

---

parisons; Farr and others (1971), seventeen comparisons, one of which was not counted since correlations were negative for both blacks and whites; Reschly and Sabers (1979), ten comparisons; Cleary (1968), one comparison; Centra and others (1970), one comparison; Kallingal (1971), five comparisons; Pfeifer and Sedlacek (1971), four comparisons; Goldman and Hewitt (1976), two comparisons; and Silverman, Barton, and Lyon (1976), two comparisons.

*If we assume that an ability is unidimensional, the probability of a correct response can be expressed as a logistic function of true ability, 0. This function has three parameters, one of which is analogous to the classical item difficulty parameter and another of which is analogous to the classical item discrimination parameter. The third parameter is the lower asymptote of the curve and corresponds to the probability that those at very low levels of ability will answer the item correctly. For multiple-choice items, this is often conceptualized as the probability of obtaining a correct response by guessing. Details of these models and their application to measurement problems can be found in Lord (1980).

ity must be considered unproved at this point. The special case, however, where a test is valid only for whites, not for blacks—sometimes called single-group validity—does not appear to be supported by the literature. The correlations for blacks were not significantly greater than zero in only four of the fifty-three comparisons just cited, and of those, one was not valid for whites, either. While the aptitude tests surveyed by these studies may not have equal "true" validity in predicting later achievement for blacks and whites, the tests do appear to be valid in predicting later achievement for black examinees.

Construct Validity Studies

A major flaw in all studies of predictive bias, whether they are regression studies or simple correlations between predictors and criteria, is that the criterion measures are apt to be biased to an unknown degree. Williams, Mosby, and Hinson (1978) argue that predictive validity in such studies is maximized when the degree of bias in the test and the degree of bias in the criterion are closely matched. Lower validities result if there is more bias in the criterion than in the test or vice versa. Although these authors state their argument in quite different terms, their formulation resembles the criticisms made by Darlington (1971). Flaugher (1978) also has raised the question of the adequacy of the criterion for reflecting the ability that we wish to measure. "No one," he states, "really believes in the superiority of the traditional college's freshman-year grade point average or in the inviolability of supervisory ratings of job performance. Yet their presence is everywhere in these studies, like an unwelcome guest being ignored with enthusiasm" (Flaugher, 1978, p. 676).(Gulliksen [1976] has a detailed discussion of criterion validity.) The reliability of the criterion measure relative to the reliability of the test can also affect the outcome of a bias analysis.

Problems created by the need for unbiased measures of ability are not the only difficulty posed by predictive studies of bias. Criterion measures are unavailable in many instances for which bias is of interest, or else they are too expensive to collect. Moreover, as Jensen (1980) points out, the validity of intelligence tests does not depend on their prediction of specific criteria. Shepard (in press) argues that, although prediction of later performance is one use for tests, a test score can also be said to be used as soon as it is interpreted. Consequently, it can be argued that tests need to be studied without reference to outside criteria. That is, we need studies to establish that test scores have the same meaning for two groups of interest.

Analysis of Factor Structure. One means of investigating whether scores have the same meaning for different groups is to examine their factor structure. In general, studies comparing factor structure of aptitude tests for blacks and for whites have shown that patterns of factor loadings are the same for both groups (Gutkin and Reynolds, 1981; Hennessy and Merrifield, 1976; Jensen, 1980; Miele, 1979; Reschly, 1978). When differences were found, they tended to be in the magnitude of the loadings (Hennessy and Merrifield,

1976; Jensen, 1980). In these cases, factor loadings were smaller for blacks, which suggests that the particular factor was less clearly delineated within the black group than within the white group or alternately that there was more error or specific variance in the scores of blacks than in the scores of whites.

In the Hennessy and Merrifield study (1976), oblique factor rotation was used so that correlations among factors would also be obtained. This study examined the factor structure of the Comparative Guidance and Placement Program battery (College Entrance Examination Board, 1970). Three factors were extracted: a verbal factor, which included measures of vocabulary, reading comprehension, and grammatical skills and usage; a reasoning factor; and a spatial-relationship factor. The verbal factor was found to be more highly correlated with the other two factors extracted for the black group than it was for the other groups studied. Several tests in this battery, however, used tasks and item types that were quite novel, in an attempt to obtain measures of reasoning ability. The authors concluded that, "As a minimum level of verbal competence was a prerequisite for measuring other special abilities using the types of tests included in this study, the apparent differences in structure may result from the combined facilitating and differentiating effects of verbal abilities" (Hennessy and Merrifield, 1976, p. 759). It might be added that, for novel tasks, much of the verbal load comes in the instructions, which must be comprehended before the requisite reasoning abilities can be applied and a solution reached.

Reschly (1978) gave results slightly different from the overall findings of similarity of factor structure. He factor analyzed the WISC-R for four ethnic groups: blacks, whites, Chicanos, and Native American Papago children. When two factors were extracted from the data, the results were essentially the same for all groups both for magnitude and for patterns of factor loadings. For the three-factor solution, the data clearly supported the extraction of a third factor only for whites, although the third factor extracted for Chicanos was similar both to the third factor extracted for whites and to the third factor found in Kaufman's (1975) factor analysis of the WISC-R. For blacks and Papagos, however, the third factor appeared to result from a splitting of the second factor found in the two-factor solution into two factors, and it was clearly different both from the third factor Reschly obtained for whites and Chicanos and from the third obtained by Kaufman (1975). In the Gutkin and Reynolds study (1981), the third factor also failed to meet the traditional "eigenvalue greater than one" criterion, although the resultant factor loadings did, in this case, closely resemble those for whites. Although this finding only suggests that there are process differences for blacks and whites, it is provocative to note that the meaning of this third factor, even for whites, is not completely clear (Kaufman, 1975).

A different approach was used by Church, Pine, and Weiss (1978). They did not analyze intact tests but collections of items like those used in standard aptitude tests. Three tests were developed and separately factor analyzed at the item level. The vocabulary test included a number of items drawn from black literature sources and designated *black-type* words. Analyses were based on matrices of phi coefficients, with the important factors rotated orthoonally. Since factor analyses at the item level are less stable than factor analyses of tests scores, it is probably not surprising that there was less similarity of factor loadings here than in the other studies cited. In general, the same number of factors were extracted for both blacks and whites, and the first factor accounted for more variance for whites than for blacks on all three item sets. Only the mathematics items showed a clear similarity of factor structure. In both the vocabulary and spatial item sets, the largest factor extracted for whites was not extracted for blacks. In both cases, the first factor for blacks appeared to coincide with the second factor for whites. Among the vocabulary items, the first factor for whites appeared to be associated with the black vocabulary words. Unfortunately, no other attempt was made to interpret the factors or to explore the reasons for the differences obtained.

Confirmatory factor analysis was used by Rock and Werts (1979) and by Rock, Werts, and Grandy (1980) to study factor structure in the SAT and the Graduate Record Examination (GRE), respectively. In these analyses, the hypotheses to be confirmed included equivalent factor structure for blacks and whites, equal scale units of measurement, equal standard errors of measurement, and equal reliabilities. These analyses are of particular interest here, since they should reflect some of the effects of the statistical bias hypothesized in this chapter. In their study of the GRE, the hypothesis of equivalent factor structure was not rejected, but the hypothesis of equal measurement units was. The authors concluded that, since the sample sizes were large and the apparent effect size was small, this should be treated as if it was not a significant result; thus the testing of the other hypotheses was considered appropriate, and it was done. Likewise, in the study of the SAT, even the hypothesis of equal factor structure was rejected for the verbal tests, but the effect was again judged to be small and the other hypotheses were tested; all hypotheses showed significant chi-square values. The argument of the investigators that the chi-square values would be significant for any trivial deviation for their sample, however, is refuted by the fact that several of the chi-square values reported are insignificant. None of the hypotheses was rejected for the SAT math except the final tests for standard error of measurement and reliability. In the GRE study, two of the five chi-squares were insignificant, with associated probabilities of .75 and .999. The authors of these two studies implicitly defined bias as differential validity, and from this perspective, the decrements in validity that could result from these differences in measurement properties would probably not in themselves be large. The significance tests do suggest, however, that these measurement properties are not in fact identical and that the analyses do provide evidence of bias of the sort hypothesized in this chapter.

In the study of the GRE (Rock, Werts, and Grandy, 1980), evidence was also found of interactions between groups and item types. The test was divided into subscales, with two scales defined for each of the ten item types used. These items were assumed to be measures of three underlying abilities; verbal, quantitative, and analytic. A three-factor solution corresponding to these abilities was found to fit the data less well than a four-factor solution, where the reading items defined the fourth factor. This reading factor was found to correlate more highly with the analytic factor than with the verbal factor that it was intended to measure, which suggests a heavy reading component to these tests. Of the three analytic item types, the analysis of explanation items appeared to produce lower factor scores for blacks than could be expected if these item types were measuring the same analytic ability as the other item types. Again, the instructions accompanying these items were extremely complex.

The results of the factor analytic studies generally appear to support the similarity of factor structure for blacks and whites and hence the essential validity of the tests. However, these studies also reach findings which suggest that other processes may operate differentially for blacks and whites. These processes may be valid aspects of the ability being measured, or they may contribute to error variance or to bias in the statistical sense defined here. That is, these processes may contribute to systematic bias or inaccuracy in the estimation of true ability for one or the other or for both of two racial groups.

Analysis of Item Difficulty. Another means of examining the relations within a test is to examine the patterns of item difficulty. The procedures used for this are similar to the methods used to study item bias, in that they focus on item statistics, but the purpose is different. The patterns of item difficulty are examined for evidence of bias in the test, while the item bias procedures seek to identify items that may contribute to bias. The procedures for examining patterns of difficulty can be divided into two broad categories. One category is represented primarily by the techniques proposed by Jensen (1974, 1976, 1977, 1980) for comparing item difficulties or other item statistics. The second uses analysis of variance approaches to look for item-by-group interactions, as proposed by Cardall and Coffman (1964) and by Cleary and Hilton (1968).

One procedure suggested by Jensen obtains the rank-order correlation of the item difficulty values obtained by two groups. Jensen uses this procedure in examining the Raven's Progressive Matrices, the Peabody Picture Vocabulary Test, and the Wonderlic Personnel Test and cites this information for the Stanford-Binet (Jensen, 1976, 1980). Miele (1979) provides similar evidence for the Wechsler Intelligence Scale for Children (WISC). In all cases, the rank-order correlations are very high. Even if the test is basically valid, the problem with this technique is that the rank-order correlation is not particularly sensitive to shifts in item difficulty for individual items.

To illustrate this and other problems that will be discussed later, I generated several sets of simulated item difficulty values. The tests so generated differed in length and in the distribution of item difficulty; that is, some tests had peaked distributions of difficulty values, and others had rectangular distributions. The peaked tests were generated with item difficulties (proportion passing) selected from a normal distribution with mean .65 and standard ·deviation .12. These values were chosen to represent a multiple-choice test of approximately middle difficulty (for four-option items) and to ensure that values would remain within the usual range for test item difficulties. For the rectangular distribution, values were selected from a uniform distribution constrained to lie between .20 and 1.00. The long test had 161 items (the number analyzed by Miele, 1979), the medium, 40 items, and the short, 10 items. The resultant distributions are rather extreme, being alternately more peaked or more flat than the distributions that would be seen for most tests. Two biased sets of item difficulties were then generated for each test by subtracting a randomly determined bias quantity from each of the item values. This quantity had a mean of .12 and a standard deviation equal to one quarter or one half of the standard deviation of item difficulties in the original, unbiased test — approximately .12 for the peaked tests and .24 for the rectangular. Both product-moment and rank-order correlations were obtained between the unbiased item set and each of the two biased item sets for each combination of test length and item difficulty distribution.

The results are shown in Table 1. For the smaller bias quantity (one-quarter standard deviation), none of the correlations is seriously affected. For peaked tests, none fell below .90, while for tests with rectangular distributions none fell below .97. The larger degree of bias did have noticeable effects on the correlations but only for the peaked tests. For the rectangular item distribution, the correlations were lower with the higher degree of bias, but none of the correlations was below .90, although item discrepancies were as large as .49 (where the mean discrepancy was .12).

The studies reporting rank-order correlations of items usually give test length, but they provide no information on the distribution of items. In the case of the WISC data, Jensen (1976) suggests that the varied content of the items across the entire WISC battery implies that lower rank-order correlations should be found. In fact, the rank-order correlations between ps (proportion passing) for different racial groups reported by Miele range from .82 to .97, with a median of .93. The spread of item difficulty in this test however, is very large, in order to provide material over a sufficiently wide range of mental development to provide measurement over several years of childhood growth. Moreover, because of the very wide range of difficulty, only those items judged to be of an appropriate level are actually administered. Hence, for children of a given age group, the chances are that some items were never administered (as too easy) or answered correctly by all examinees and that others were never administered (as too difficult) or answered incorrectly by all examinees. The presence of such items in group comparisons could lead to overestimates of the rank-order correlations. In fact, all the correlations reported by Miele that were below .90 were for cross-age comparisons. Within a single age group, where the shared number of zero and one difficulties might

Table 1. Product-Moment and Rank-Order Correlations on Simulated Data Reflecting Varying Degrees of Bias

Test Length	Degree of Bias[a]	Mean	Standard Deviation	Range hi	Range lo	Correlation r	Correlation rho
			Peaked Test				
Short	unbiased	.62	.12	.87	.48		
	1/4 sd	.51	.12	.75	.34	.978	.997
	1/2 sd	.51	.13	.73	.40	.914	.742
Medium	unbiased	.62	.10	.89	.43		
	1/4 sd	.51	.10	.75	.31	.942	.906
	1/2 sd	.51	.12	.84	.27	.890	.854
Long	unbiased	.65	.12	.91	.26		
	1/4 sd	.54	.12	.81	.14	.968	.958
	1/2 sd	.54	.13	.90	.16	.889	.878
			Uniform Test				
Short	unbiased	.58	.22	.99	.27		
	1/4 sd	.47	.21	.89	.15	.977	.988
	1/2 sd	.47	.26	.94	.13	.934	.927
Medium	unbiased	.58	.23	.99	.22		
	1/4 sd	.45	.23	.90	.07	.970	.999
	1/2 sd	.45	.27	1.00	-.05	.902	.998
Long	unbiased	.62	.24	.99	.20		
	1/4 sd	.50	.25	.97	.02	.974	.971
	1/2 sd	.49	.27	1.10	-.09	.907	.916

[a]Bias was introduced by subtracting a "bias quantity" from each item difficulty value in the unbiased test, with a mean of .12 and a standard deviation equal to one quarter or one half of the standard deviation of the unbiased item difficulty values. For the peaked tests, these values were .03 and .06, respectively, and for the uniform test, .06 and .12.

be largest, the rank-order correlations ranged from .90 to .97, with a median of .94. Even with the simulated data and the somewhat restricted number of items with proportions correct in the range between zero and one, however, the correlations reported by Miele appear to be consistent with the presence of biased items in the test when compared with the simulated data.

Angoff and Ford (1973) also correlated item difficulties for the Preliminary Scholastic Aptitude Test (PSAT), using product-moment correlations and item delta values (normal deviates corresponding to the obtained percent correct, converted to a scale with mean 13 and standard deviation 4). The range of obtained correlations between deltas over a number of differently defined black and white groups was similar to that obtained by Miele, .79 to .99. However, Angoff and Ford also compared randomly selected groups that were both all black or both all white so that correlations of deltas for groups that were not different could be compared with correlations of deltas for groups that were different. They also compared groups that were both black but that differed in urban or rural orientation as well as in test score and groups that differed in race but that matched on scores.

The delta values for two racially homogeneous groups were quite similar, although they were generally more similar for whites than they were for blacks. Only four correlations were obtained between groups of white candidates, and these were all .97 or higher. The correlations between black groups for the verbal tests ranged between .92 and .98 and for the math, between .92 and .97, with a median of .95 for both. The correlations between groups ranged between .89 and .96, with a median of .94, for the verbal tests and between .79 and .92, with a median of .88, for the math tests. However, some of this difference appears to be due to the differences in mean overall performance between the two groups. When scores were matched on the alternate tests, the correlation between verbal deltas for blacks and whites matched on math scores was .96, and the correlation for math deltas where groups were matched on verbal scores was .92. In contrast, correlations of delta values between urban and rural blacks, where mean performance differences were also large, ranged between .92 and .96 for verbal and between .92 and .95 for math. In general, although the correlations within groups were higher than correlations between groups for both math and verbal items, the explanation that the lower correlations for the verbal items were due to group mean differences in score is at least tenable. However, in the case of the math items, the distributions of correlations between and within groups were almost nonoverlapping. The lowest within-group correlation and the highest between-group correlation were both .92. Furthermore, the within-group distributions of correlations for the math and verbal tests were essentially the same, even for black groups differing in urbal or rural background. In contrast, the correlations between groups for the two tests were quite different, with correlations for the math tests markedly lower. Consequently, the math reasoning subtests of the PSAT do appear to be biased under this definition.

The analysis of variance procedures provide a more systematic approach to patterns of item difficulty. These procedures yield main effects due to group performance differences or to differences in item difficulty and an interaction effect between group and items. A significant item-by-group interaction implies that the patterns of item difficulty are different for the two groups. These procedures have been used by Jensen in the study of the Peabody Picture Vocabulary Test, and Raven's Progressive Matrices, and the Wonderlic Personnel Test (1974, 1977, 1980); by Cardall and Coffman (1964) with the SAT; by Cleary and Hilton (1968) with the PSAT; by Miele (1979) with the WISC; and by Cotter and Berk (1981) with the WISC-R. In all cases, all interactions were significant for unselected groups of examinees, where group main effects tend to be large.

When groups were selected to be more nearly equivalent in score, main effects were much reduced—often insignificant—and the magnitude of the interactions was also reduced. Jensen reported nonsignificant interactions for selected groups on the three tests that he studied, while the interactions for the WISC (Miele, 1979) were much reduced but remained significant. In the Cotter and Berk study (1981), only learning disabled children were in the sample, with the result that overall ethnic group differences were not significant. Significant interactions were obtained, however, on four of the nine subtests examined: Information, Similarities, Comprehension, and Picture Completion. In general, the significant interactions in these studies, when reported, were in the neighborhood of 1 percent of the variance accounted for, although Miele's study (1979) accounted for variance ranging from 2.4 to 4.2 percent in his unselected groups. Since the largest part of the variance is accounted for by differences in item difficulty, the percent of variance that could be accounted for by the interaction, even in a very biased test, is not apt to be large.

There are several problems with these procedures for studying patterns of item difficulty in the assessment of bias. One problem is that the item difficulty patterns are confounded with item discrimination, that is, the ability of an item to distinguish between individuals or between groups that differ in ability. When the groups being compared differ both in the ability that is being measured and in background variables, such as race, sex, or socioeconomic status, items that are discriminating to a much greater or much lesser extent than other items in the test will contribute to item-by-group interactions. Hence, much of the reduction of this interaction for selected groups comes from the removal of the effect of these differences in item discrimination. However, an item that is satisfactory for whites but completely nondiscriminating for blacks can make no contribution to the interaction if the mean between-group difference in item performance for such an item is similar to that for the other items in the test. One could easily argue, however, that such an item is biased under the definition that we are using here.

Another problem is illustrated by the example of simulated data in Table 1. Notice that a change in the standard deviation of the bias attached to the item values has some effect on the correlations and perhaps makes some slight difference in the resulting standard deviation of item difficulties. The mean of the biased item difficulties remains essentially unchanged, however, with the relatively large change in the amount of bias added to individual items. That is, only the mean of the bias quantity is reflected in the differences in item performance, while the variance of that quantity has almost no effect. In the various procedures just discussed, however, the mean bias quantity is treated as if it were a true ability difference, and only the variability of this quantity would be detected as bias. In the analysis of variance, any difference between scores or item performances that results from bias is treated as part of the main effect. Hence, a test that presents all items in a format that is more difficult for blacks than for whites of the same ability and for which the items are relatively equivalent in discrimination will appear to be unbiased when analyzed by any of these procedures. This objection also holds for the item bias procedures, but because these methods are designed rather to isolate items for further study than to discover bias in tests, they pose a less serious problem for interpretation of the results of studies that use them than the item pattern methods do.

Item Bias Results

Most recent studies of test item bias have been directed at developing and validating procedures for detecting items that are biased against the groups of concern. As noted earlier in this chapter, most procedures can be placed in one of two large categories — procedures related to the item-by-group interaction definition of bias and procedures that are conditional on the ability of examinees. Unlike the regression approaches to test bias, several of which lead to mutually contradictory results, the item bias procedures have generally been shown to produce convergent results (Ironson and Subkoviak, 1979; Nungester, 1977; Rudner, 1977; Shepard, Camilli, and Averill, 1981). Studies using these procedures have shown that, although the agreement is far from perfect, the indices derived from various techniques do tend to covary, at least when based on one of the two major conceptualizations of item bias discussed here.

These procedures have also been shown to distinguish between differences associated with group membership and differences in performance. Rudner (1977) formed pseudogroups consisting entirely of majority group examinees who showed the same differences in score distributions as his groups of interest. (In his study, persons with normal hearing were compared to persons whose hearing was impaired.) Using three methods derived from one of the two major definitions, he found little if any bias reflected in the items studied for the pseudogroups. In contrast, a large number of the same items appeared to be biased for the hearing impaired. A fourth procedure, based on a different formulation of bias, failed to show this distinction between groups varying only in scores and groups defined by the variable of interest. In another study, Rudner, Getson, and Knight (1980b) simulated biased items, again using Birnbaum's three-parameter latent trait model. They found that bias indices derived from the methods studied correlated with the degree of bias built into the items.

The bias that has been found to exist in items, however, has not been clearly tied to bias in tests. In general, while the presence of biased items seems to decrease the likelihood that the test as a whole is unbiased, failure to detect item bias cannot conversely be considered as evidence that bias does not exist but only that, if bias exists, the amount of bias is much the same for all items. (See Scheuneman, in press, for examples.) Similarly, conclusions cannot be drawn from the number of biased items detected by using these procedures. Generally, we could expect these methods to rank the degree of bias detected in individual items, with some point then chosen, more or less arbitrarily, as the threshold beyond which items should be considered biased. However, appropriate methods for setting such arbitrary cutoff points, whether through statistical significance tests or other means, have not generally been agreed upon. The items selected using one of the item bias procedures can only be said to be most biased according to a definition specified for the sample being examined.

In focusing on individual items, however, the item bias procedures give us the potential — not yet well exploited in the research — for obtaining information about difficulties that may be encountered by minority examinees in responding to the items and about other possible reasons for the observed differences. In contrast, the results of studies of bias in a predictive or construct validity sense inform us about bias in a particular test, but, with the exception of certain of the factor studies, they fail to shed any light on how bias operates or on the processes that affect the scores of different groups in different ways.

One reason for the failure to make better use of the information yielded by studies of item bias is the frequent inability of researchers to interpret the results obtained. Angoff and Ford (1973) were unable to interpret their results for the PSAT, Lord (1977) could not form meaningful explanations for items selected from the SAT, and Wightman (1979) was unable to offer an interpretation of his results for the Law School Admissions Test. Elsewhere (Scheuneman, in press), I have discussed in detail the interpretation of item bias results. Here, I will only repeat some of the reasons why I believe investigators have failed to find interpretations for their results.

One problem in inferring possible causes of the item bias results arises from the common expectation that the major, if not the only, source of differential performance concerns the relative familiarity or unfamiliarity of black examinees with the item content. Cotter and Berk (1981) report that such explanations were offered by a panel of black reviewers for some items on the WISC-R identified as biased. Ironson and Subkoviak (1979) report an item on the National Longitudinal Survey exam apparently favoring blacks that was set in a black context. Similarly, Conrad and Wallmark (1975) report GRE reading passages with black content that appear to favor blacks. Ironson and Subkoviak further report that items concerning money, with the use of which all examinees should be equally familiar, apparently favor blacks. I also observed with the Otis-Lennon School Ability Test (Scheuneman, 1978) that items involving money tended to be relatively easier than math reasoning items set in other terms. For the majority of cases, however, such explanations cannot be found.

Another difficulty, even when such content differences exist, is that cutting points on the bias indices are set in such a way that relatively few items are identified as potentially biased. Potential causes can often be detected because of similarities among certain of the items identified. Particularly in the case of verbal items, any of a large number of different elements in the item can be the source of the bias detected. A finding that items identified as biased have certain elements in common leads us to focus on possible causes that may otherwise go undetected. If only a small number of items have been identified for study, the possibilities of detecting such similarities are much reduced.

The format in which an item is presented is another possible cause of the bias detected, and it is more or less independent of content and context.

Such sources of bias cannot be detected, however, unless more than one item format has been used to measure the underlying ability. In a study using pretest data for the Otis-Lennon (Scheuneman, 1978), I had responses to 480 items administered to pupils in grades 8 and 9 and to 240 other items administered to pupils in grades 11 and 12. The items were intended to measure verbal comprehension, verbal reasoning, quantitative reasoning, and figural (spatial) reasoning. Fourteen item formats were used for grades 8 and 9, and twelve formats were used for grades 11 and 12. In both item sets, analogies were identified as biased more often than other verbal reasoning items, and figural series items were selected as biased more often than figural items presented in other formats. Among measures of quantitative reasoning, letter series were also more often identified as biased. Letter series, however, may measure something different from the other quantitative items if the misclassification results in a preponderance of such items' being identified as potentially biased within the quantitative set.

For measures of verbal ability, three formats have been examined often enough that I was able to locate three studies, which used different bias procedures and different tests, that reported results for these formats. In my study of the Otis-Lennon pretest (1978), Stricker's study of the GRE (1981), and Echternacht's study of the Admission Test for Graduate Study in Business (1972), results were reported for antonyms, analogies, and sentence-completion items. Echternacht's study included only fourteen items of each type; Stricker had between seventeen and twenty items of each type; while I had forty-two antonyms, thirty-six sentence completions, and sixty-six analogies for grades 8 and 9 and twenty-four antonyms, twenty-one sentence completions, and thirty-nine analogies for grades 11 and 12.

Stricker and Echternacht analyzed the comparison between blacks and whites separately by sex and found no format differences among these item types for females. For males, however, both found that a preponderance of items identified as potentially biased were antonyms. In the Otis-Lennon, high levels of antonyms were identified as biased only for grades 8 and 9. For grades 11 and 12, 25 percent of the antonym items were identified as biased, but this may be contrasted to the 33 percent of the overall items that was identified as biased for this level. Very few sentence-completion items were identified as biased. Only the Otis-Lennon data for grades 11 and 12 showed large numbers of biased items of this type. For analogies, both levels of the Otis-Lennon data and the GRE (Stricker, 1981) data showed high proportions of biased items. Thus, the results of these three studies suggest that antonyms and analogies are likely to have many high indices of item bias and that sentence completion items show relatively few high indices.

Like some results of the factor studies, some item bias results point to inadequacies in the test instructions as possible sources of bias. For example, in the Otis-Lennon pretests, both figural and letter series items appeared to be more difficult for blacks than could be expected. Inspection of the tests showed that the item was adequate only to label the task and that no sample item had been provided to illustrate what was required. Hence, the examinee who did not understand that the word *series* implied that a kind of progression was being formed would have difficulty responding appropriately to the item. Consequently, instructions were revised, and a sample series item was provided.

In her study of the Graduate Management Admission Test, Sinnott (1980) describes a subtest concerning practical business judgment. The items in this test related to a reading passage, and the response options were the same for all items. The items consisted of statements that candidates had to classify as a major objective, a major factor in making a decision, a minor factor in the decision, a major assumption, or an unimportant issue. Results suggested that blacks may not have understood fully what test developers meant by the classification terms, which were only briefly described in the instructions. Her recommendation was that the instructions should be revised to make the definition of these terms more explicit.

One last finding, which is probably unrelated to features of the specific items identified as biased, concerns speededness. Using the usual kinds of criteria (percent completing the test and so forth), Sinnott (1980) reported differences in speededness, but she also identified the last two items in the Data Sufficiency test as biased. She interpreted this result as due to differential completion rates between whites and minority groups. Ironson and Subkoviak (1979) also noted that several identified items occurred at the end of tests.

In a broad way, the results of the various item bias studies that I have reviewed suggest that a focus on the relative familiarity of item or test content as a source of test bias is too restrictive to explain test bias in any major way. This conclusion follows both from studies in which the author failed to identify causes for bias and studies that identified differences associated with item format and other properties of the test not specific to individual items. This point will be discussed in more detail in the following sections of this chapter.

Reconceptualizing Bias

I have considered two aspects of test bias in this chapter: bias as invalidity of measurement, and bias in the statistical sense of systematic errors in estimation of the true ability of minority group examinees. The evidence from a large number of studies that used different approaches and conceptualizations appears to support the contention that the use of aptitude tests to assess blacks is essentially as valid as the use of aptitude tests to assess whites, although the validity may not be strictly equal for the two groups in specific instances. The evidence for bias in the statistical sense is less clear. For the remainder of this chapter, therefore, I will focus on this second aspect of bias, the underestimation of ability.

Let us begin by conceptualizing a multifaceted bias effect, made up of several parts, each of which is associated with some feature of the testing situation, whether it be the item, the instructions, the examiner, or the attitudes, motivations, or other predispositions of the examinee. These parts may be related to each other and to the test in complex ways, and these relationships may be different for two groups as the result of factors associated with group membership. Let us then assume that these parts form a composite that is, in theory, measurable, so that values can be obtained for a mean and standard deviation across people and across items. The model for a test score for a single ability trait would then look like this:

$X = \psi + \beta + \delta$, where
   X = the observed score,
   ψ = the true score,
   β = the bias factor, and
   δ = measurement error independent of group membership.

The expected value for δ would be zero, as in the usual true score measurement model, but the mean of β for blacks would be less than zero,* which would act to depress the observed scores below their true mean, that is, to produce statistical bias.

If this β factor exists, how does it relate to the evidence provided by the bias studies reviewed earlier? Presumably, this bias quantity could be detected with studies of predictive or concurrent validity if an unbiased criterion measure of true ability was available. In practice, however, the criterion measure used is also apt to be biased to an unknown degree. Hence, the magnitude of the differences between predicted and observed scores is most likely to be a function of the difference between the bias factor in the test and the bias factor in the criterion. Equal regressions could then occur even with biased tests, if the bias in both the test and the criterion is of similar magnitude. In the studies that I have reviewed, however, the hypothesis of equal regression was rejected sufficiently often to suggest that bias operates in the tests studied to a different degree than it operates in the criterion measures used. Thus, the evidence from these studies is more consistent with the hypothesis of a bias factor than it is with the hypothesis of no bias.

In studies where no external measure of ability is available, the mean effect of bias cannot be separated from the effect of true score differences. When we deal with people in groups, we implicitly choose to disregard the individual differences in β within ethnic groups, so the mean bias effect is absorbed into the apparent mean score difference. Likewise, the mean bias effect across items appears as part of the apparent differences between groups in item difficulty. What remains to be detected is only the variation across items. If this

---

*It would also be possible for the mean value of β to be greater than zero for whites, which would cause their scores to be overestimated; I have seen results that suggest to me that this is true. For the sake of simplicity, however, I will restrict the argument to the one direction.

variation is small compared to the mean bias factor, the effect size will appear to be quite small, perhaps insignificant, although the true bias can still be quite large. Evidence for variation in the degree of bias across items is provided by studies of item bias and item difficulty patterns. Typically, the studies of item-by-group interactions have shown significant results, although the effects have been so small that they have often been dismissed as evidence of bias. The correlations among item difficulties are generally high but within a range of values consistent with the presence of items that are differentially difficult for blacks and whites. Item bias studies have not only identified particular items that perform differently for blacks and whites, but they also have provided information about why such variation might occur. A hypothesis of no bias does not account for this variation.

Another type of evidence comes from the item bias studies that use delta plots or another of the procedures based on the item-by-group interaction definition. All items identified as biased by these methods can be interpreted as favoring one or the other of the two groups being compared. A common result is that the number of items favoring each group tends to be approximately equal. Of the studies using one of these procedures, only three of those cited here reported the presumed direction of the bias in their results, but these will serve as examples. Cotter and Berk (1981) found seven items that appeared to be biased against blacks and six that seemed to favor them. Sinnott (1980) reported results at two levels of disparity. Of the more extreme items, nine were for blacks, and eight were against blacks, while at the less restrictive level, fifteen items were for blacks, and ten were against. For the three groups that she studied, twenty of the more extreme items favored the high-scoring group, and seventeen favored the low-scoring group; at the less restrictive level, twenty-five items favored the high-scoring group, and twenty-one items favored the low-scoring group. Stricker (1981) reported very few items selected using deltas, but these divided five and three on the original test and six and four on the replication. Using other data that he provided, we can compare a less restrictive group of items, which splits six and six on the original analysis and seven and nine on the replicated analysis.

If a test is assumed to be essentially unbiased, with only a few items contributing to item-by-group interaction, there is no a priori reason to expect such symmetry. Certainly, it seems unlikely that test developers just happen by chance to write approximately equal numbers of items that favor particular groups. When such symmetry is noted, it is usually dismissed as an artifact of the method. In contrast, however, such an effect could be predicted from the formulation that I am presenting here. If the bias quantity in each item was distributed about a mean bias amount for the test, item-by-group interaction effects could be expected to center approximately at that mean, as discussed earlier, and to identify the items most extreme from it in either direction as biased. In such cases, there is a high likelihood that the number of items at some distance from the mean will be about the same in either direction. More important, however, these two sets of assumptions—that the test is essentially unbiased, or that, on the average, the test is biased to some degree against blacks—lead to somewhat different interpretations of items that appear to favor blacks when these procedures are used. Depending on the unknown value of the mean bias quantity, items with bias values that are the farthest below that mean can in reality be items that favor blacks, but they can also be items with little or no bias or even the items with the least amount of bias against blacks. The assumption of no bias yields only one interpretation of these findings—bias favoring blacks—or else, in view of the unnatural symmetry, it rejects these findings as methodological artifacts.

Another kind of evidence from the bias studies relates to the possible sources of bias. One possible source of bias is item content. Critics of testing are especially prone to cite items that call for knowledge which is apt to be outside the usual experiences of many black examinees, such as knowledge of art or classical music. Jensen (1980) musters impressive evidence to refute this hypothesis as any but a minor source of differential test performance. Item bias research, which he does not cite, has failed to identify any large number of items that can be interpreted in this way. Viewed in terms of the model presented here, such factors can be seen as specific to the items on which they appear and hence as contributors to the variation across items and perhaps, in the aggregate, to mean differences. These surface properties, which are easily identified as associated with culture, should not, however, be considered the only culturally loaded portions of the test.

Jackson (1975, p. 92) stated it this way: "The process of constructing tests that uses different items but employs the same logic, structure, and other similar features renders [some] promising approaches . . . ineffective and maintains the bias." Bernal (1975, p. 93) questioned the validity of the test for those "who may be psychometrically naive, those lacking experience with tests generally and not accustomed to dealing with information in ways required by a particular instrument." These statements can be supported, at least in part, by the results of item bias studies that show bias to be associated with particular item formats or with methods by which the abilities are to be measured. In many ways, the testing instrument itself and the testing activity that uses these instruments must be seen as manifestations of white middle-class scholarship, thought, and values. Anastasi (1976, p. 345) reminds us that "the mere use of paper and pencil in the presentation of abstract tasks having no immediate significance will favor some cultural groups and handicap others."

Nonetheless, minority examinees, in the main, do respond appropriately to testing instruments in ways that, to a large extent, maintain the same relationships among scores and between scores and criteria that characterize the responses of whites. I hypothesize, however, that the demands placed on examinees by making a correct response are greater for blacks and other minorities than they are for middle-class whites. The effect of these greater demands is to reduce the probability of a correct response for a person of a given ability; that is, they bias the results.

Evidence of such differences in demand requirements can be found in a variety of places. One way in which the demand can be different is in requiring the use of nonoptimal strategies; another way is in requiring examinees to develop strategies for responding to items during the testing itself rather than allowing examinees to use previously learned strategies. In both cases, the speed with which the examinee completes a test can be affected. In general, the study of speededness in tests is a complex topic. In reference to comparative studies of speededness in groups, Rindler (1979, p. 262) stated that "these have been undermined both by the murkiness of the theoretical literature on test speededness and by the resulting inadequacy of currently applied measures of speed."

Some evidence of the effects of speed is provided in the studies by Ironson and Subkoviak (1979) and Sinnott (1980); in these studies, items at the end of the test showed sufficient differences in performance between blacks and whites to allow the tests to be identified as biased. Sinnott also demonstrated substantial differences in the proportion of blacks and whites who completed the exam. Some of the complexities of this issue have been illustrated in a study by Evans (1980). Although he was unable to demonstrate differential effects of speededness, he found that white examinees who completed a short test made up of SAT items had higher overall scores than those who did not complete the test, while the reverse was true for black examinees. Among blacks, those who did not complete the test earned higher scores. In general, the material was quite difficult, and the blacks who completed the test appeared to be responding inappropriately or with little thought, while blacks who responded correctly to many items did not finish the test.

Evidence suggesting that blacks may be using different processes or strategies in responding to test items comes from two studies concerning fluid and crystallized intelligence. Schmidt and Crano (1974) used a cross-lagged panel analysis to test the hypothesis that fluid ability acts as a cause of crystallized ability in children of both lower- and middle-socioeconomic status. This hypothesis was confirmed only for the middle-class group. Cattell and Horn (1978) also examined this relationship, using two groups even more diverse — one made up of black, rural children, mainly of low socioeconomic status, and the other of white, urban, middle-class children. Again, the hypothesis concerning the relationship between fluid and crystallized abilities was confirmed only for the middle-class group. The authors concluded (Cattell and Horn, 1978, p. 160): "Under the conditions of living that exist for the children of [the black] sample — rural, slum, few incentives associated with academic, as compared to other, achievement, and so on — the major determinant of academic performance and performance on a standard IQ test is fluid intelligence," not crystallized intelligence, as was the case for the more advantaged group. If different fundamental abilities are required in order to respond to the items on aptitude tests, as these two studies suggest, the tasks set by these items cannot be considered fully equivalent for both groups.

Green (1972) provides evidence for the difference of the tests for blacks and whites from the perspective of test construction. This study used achievement test data, but similar results could be expected for data from aptitude tests. Using standard items from a pretest administration of the California Achievement Test and typical criteria of item difficulty and discrimination, Green selected the best subset of items for separate groups of northern urban blacks, southern rural blacks, southwestern Mexican Americans, and whites from the same three regions. Between 30 to 40 percent of the items that were best for the black groups were different from the items selected as best for whites. In general, the performance of a given minority group was better on the test selected for it than it was on the total unselected test, but almost uniformly it was better than on the test selected for whites. The most frequent exception concerned the southern rural white group. Green (1972, p. 108) notes that "the more economically dissimilar the groups contrasted, the less likely it is that they will produce data leading to the selection of the same items." These results suggest that even among standard item types, items selected for inclusion in a test may not be items that are most effective measures for black examinees.

If the demands placed on black and white examinees are different, then modification of the demands should produce a change in the score differences. One such modification could consist of practice or instruction concerning specific item types. Whitely and Dawis (1974) report significant increases in performance on verbal analogy items for inner-city high school students following a single fifty-minute session consisting of instruction, description of item structures, and feedback on performance. They did not, however, find that practice alone was sufficient to produce a change, even when feedback was provided. Jensen (1980) cites a study by Dyer (1970) which showed that practice and special instruction sessions using aptitude-type items raised scores of blacks more than they raised scores of whites, although the magnitude of the differences was small. Unfortunately, the within-group variation of pre-existing test-taking ability is apt to be large both for blacks and whites. Since those who already possess the strategies provided by the instruction cannot be expected to show performance gains as a result, those with low ability would be the most apt to gain from such instruction, regardless of their group membership. Thus, the gains from instruction on item types could be expected to be greater for blacks, because their mean test-taking ability would be expected to be lower initially than the mean test-taking ability of whites, not because whites uniformly possess these skills and blacks uniformly do not. Consequently, small effect sizes should not be surprising. Also, the intervention periods were quite short in both cases.

A different way of changing the task demands is to change the mode of presentation. Johnson and Mihal (1973) compare paper-and-pencil and computer administrations of the School and College Ability Test (SCAT). The two parallel forms of the SCAT were given in counterbalanced order, with one form administered via a computer terminal with no feedback and the alternate form administered using the usual procedures; all items were presented in the same sequence. On the total test and on the verbal test, blacks who had the computerized administration showed significantly higher scores. In fact, there were no differences in scores between blacks and whites on the computerized verbal test, although scores on the paper-and-pencil tests showed the usual group performance differences. Pine (1977) reports a study comparing computerized and paper-and-pencil administrations of a vocabulary test. Here, two test forms were developed for each mode of administration; within each pair, bias indices were used to produce a low-bias form. Half of the examinees who took each form were also provided with feedback. The computerized tests were administered adaptively to be appropriate for the examinee's ability. The computer adaptive testing was found to be more effective than the low-bias paper-and-pencil form in reducing performance differences, and feedback was found to be more influential when provided by the computer.

The demands placed on black examinees by the so-called culture-fair tests deserve special mention here. Skanes and others (1974, p. 568) state: "The effort to make tests culture-fair by choosing novel material . . . or completely familiar material did not succeed, because test makers neglected to ensure that the relevant strategies were equally novel or equally familiar." In her discussion of problems with cross-cultural measurement, Anastasi (1976) argues that nonverbal test materials are related to cultural perceptions that are even less well understood than language differences.

The Raven's Progressive Matrices is an example of this type of test. It has been used extensively in studies of group performance differences because of its purportedly low level of cultural loading. Internal analyses of item difficulties and item-by-group interactions have suggested that the degree of bias in this test is low. Because the items of the Raven's are all presented in the same format and the content shows little item-to-item variation in familiarity or previous exposure, variation in the bias factor β is apt to be quite small. Hence, much of the variation observed in the analyses may in fact be due to differences in item discrimination. If the mode of representing relationships or the mental strategies or manipulations required by this item format are in themselves more difficult for blacks, however, the mean bias could be quite large and still produce the observed item difficulty patterns.

I would hypothesize that the demands placed on a black examinee increase with the distance of test material from the examinee's own life experience and that this distance is greater for blacks than for whites. The case of culture-fair tests represents not only material that is very abstract and devoid of real-life meaning, but the presentation of this material in a puzzle-like mode is also more distant from the experience of blacks than it is from the experience of whites. At the other extreme, there is the frequently cited WISC-R item, "What would you do if a child much smaller than yourself came up and hit you?" It has been determined that the correct response to this item contradicts the norms of the ghetto concerning fighting, but fighting is also a situation that the ghetto child knows and most likely has experienced. The distance between the child and the life experience is here very small. In fact, this item is relatively easier for blacks than it is for whites (Cotter and Berk, 1981; Jensen, 1980). Generally, in comparing verbal and nonverbal tests, the verbal materials must be considered closer to the experience of black examinees than the nonverbal materials, despite variations in individual items that make some verbal content less familiar than other. Results show that when these comparisons are made, performance differences, when they exist, most often favor the verbal over the nonverbal materials (Jensen, 1980).

Conclusions

One major purpose of this chapter was to convey the complexity of the issue of ethnic-group bias in aptitude testing. This problem will not yield to simplistic solutions or to unitary concepts of bias. I have suggested here that bias can be thought of as a multifaceted component of the observed score that, in composite, has some mean and standard deviation across people and across items. I have shown that this formulation is consistent with the results of bias studies. Next, I hypothesized that one major factor in this bias quantity was differences in the demands placed by a test or item on black and white examinees, and I provided some evidence concerning ways in which these demands can be shown to differ. Finally, I suggested that one kind of demand difference is related to the distance of the task or content, whether it be verbal or nonverbal, from the examinee's life experience, and I demonstrated that this explanation is consistent with findings relating performance on different types of items, where explanations based on verbal item content are not.

One disturbing trend found in several studies cited here was the tendency to dismiss results because of small effect sizes. For this reason, it is important to stress the multifaceted nature of bias. If we expect a single source to account for a large portion of the observed score differences, we are probably doomed to be disappointed in our efforts. If this source cannot be found, there is a tendency to conclude that the test must be unbiased or that bias is only a minor source at best of the observed differences. Researchers who are convinced that tests are unbiased may find my arguments and the evidence that I have presented paltry and unconvincing. I would assert, however, that the formulations that I have presented here are at least as consistent with the experimental results as the conclusion of no bias.

Further, I believe that it is probably premature to expect a clear explication of bias. At this time, the state of the art is such that we do not fully understand what aptitude items measure. The study of processes used in responding to these items is now an active area of research in cognitive psychology (Pellegrino and Glaser, 1980; Snow, 1980; Sternberg, 1977; Whitely, 1976). We are far from understanding why one individual uses one strategy while another individual uses a different strategy, let alone how these differences are associated with group membership. Moreover, we do not have a substantial body of knowledge describing the cultural differences between American blacks and whites, nor can we measure the variations within these groups with regard to the identification of different individuals having these cultural characteristics.

For the time being, I believe that research into item bias provides the greatest potential for future understanding of the bias issue. Such research can increase our knowledge about contributors to the variations in performance associated with group membership. Indeed, studies that identify processes associated with differential item difficulty can feed back into the more basic research concerning the processes used in responding to aptitude items. Research into bias in test items is in its infancy, but I believe that it has great potential for increasing our understanding not only of ethnic-group bias but of measurement itself.

References

Anastasi, A. *Psychological Testing.* (4th ed.) New York: Macmillan, 1976.

Angoff, W. H. "The Use of Difficulty and Discrimination Indices in the Identification of Biased Test Items." In R. A. Berk (Ed.), *Handbook of Methods for Detecting Test Bias.* Baltimore, Md.: Johns Hopkins University Press, in press.

Angoff, W. H., and Ford, S. F. "Item-Race Interaction on a Test of Scholastic Aptitude." *Journal of Educational Measurement,* 1973, *10,* 95–106.

Bernal, E. M. "A Response to 'Educational Uses of Tests with Disadvantaged Subjects.'" *American Psychologist,* 1975, *30,* 93–95.

Boehm, V. R. "Negro-White Differences in Validity of Employment and Training Selection Procedures: Summary of the Research Evidence." *Journal of Applied Psychology,* 1972, *56,* 33–39.

Cardall, C., and Coffman, W. E. *A Method for Comparing the Performance of Different Groups on the Items in a Test.* Princeton, N.J.: Educational Testing Service, 1964.

Cattell, R. B., and Horn, J. L. "A Cross-Social Check on the Theory of Fluid and Crystallized Intelligence with Discovery of New Valid Subtest Designs." *Journal of Educational Measurement,* 1978, *15,* 139–164.

Centra, J. A., Linn, R. L., and Parry, M. E. "Academic Growth in Predominantly Negro and Predominantly White Colleges." *American Educational Research Journal,* 1970, *1,* 83–98.

Church, A. T., Pine, S. M., and Weiss, D. J. *A Comparison of Levels and Dimensions of Performance in Black and White Groups on Tests of Vocabulary, Mathematics, and Spatial Ability.* Research Report 78-3. Minneapolis: Psychometric Methods Program, University of Minnesota, 1978.

Cleary, T. A. "Test Bias: Prediction of Grades of Negro and White Students in Integrated Colleges." *Journal of Educational Measurement,* 1968, *5,* 115–124.

Cleary, T. A., and Hilton, T. L. "An Investigation of Item Bias." *Educational and Psychological Measurement,* 1968, *28,* 61–75.

College Entrance Examination Board. *Comparative Guidance and Placement Program, Form SP6, 1970.* Princeton, N.J.: Educational Testing Service, 1970.

Conrad, L., and Wallmark, M. M. "Report on the Item Analysis of a GRE Aptitude Test by Ethnic and Sex Subgroups." Unpublished paper. Princeton, N.J.: Educational Testing Service, 1975.

Cotter, D. E., and Berk, R. A. "Item Bias in the WISC-R Using Black, White, and Hispanic Learning Disabled Children." Paper presented at the annual meeting of the American Educational Research Association, Los Angeles, April 1981.

Crano, W. D., Kenny, D. A., and Campbell, D. T. "Does Intelligence Cause Achievement? A Cross-Lagged Panel Analysis." *Journal of Educational Psychology*, 1972, *63*, 258–275.

Darlington, R. B. "Another Look at Cultural Fairness." *Journal of Educational Measurement*, 1971, *8*, 71–82.

Davis, J. A., and Kerner-Hoeg, S. *Validity of Preadmissions Indices for Blacks and Whites in Six Traditionally White Public Universities in North Carolina.* Princeton, N.J.: Educational Testing Service, 1971.

Dyer, P. J. "Effects of Test Conditions on Negro-White Differences in Test Scores." Unpublished doctoral dissertation, Columbia University, 1970.

Echternacht, G. *An Examination of Test Bias and Response Characteristics for Six Candidate Groups Taking the ATGSB.* Princeton, N.J.: Educational Testing Service, March 1972. (ERIC document ED 065 510)

Evans, F. R. *A Study of the Relationships Among Speed and Power Aptitude Scores and Ethnic Identity.* Princeton, N.J.: Educational Testing Service, October 1980.

Farr, J. L., O'Leary, B. S., Pfeifer, C. M., Goldstein, I. L., and Bartlett, C. J. *Ethnic-Group Membership as a Moderator in the Prediction of Job Performance: An Examination of Some Less Traditional Predictors.* Technical Report No. 2. Washington, D.C.: American Institutes for Research, 1971.

Fincher, C. "Differential Validity and Test Bias." *Personnel Psychology*, 1975, *28*, 481–500.

Flaugher, R. L. "The Many Definitions of Test Bias." *American Psychologist*, 1978, *33*, 671–679.

Goldman, R. D., and Hewitt, B. N. "Predicting the Success of Black, Chicano, Oriental, and White College Students." *Journal of Educational Measurement*, 1976, *13*, 107–117.

Goldman, R. D., and Widawski, M. H. "An Analysis of Types of Errors in the Selection of Minority College Students." *Journal of Educational Measurement*, 1976, *13*, 185–200.

Green, B. F. "In Defense of Measurement." *American Psychologist*, 1978, *33*, 664–670.

Green, D. R. *Racial and Ethnic Bias in Test Construction.* Monterey, Calif.: CTB/McGraw-Hill, 1972.

Green, R. L., and Farquhar, W. W. "Negro Academic Motivation and Scholastic Achievement." *Journal of Educational Psychology*, 1965, *56*, 241–243.

Gulliksen, H. *When High Validity May Indicate a Faulty Criterion.* Princeton, N.J.: Educational Testing Service, 1976.

Gutkin, T. B., and Reynolds, C. R. "Factorial Similarity of the WISC-R for White and Black Children from the Standardization Sample." *Journal of Educational Psychology*, 1981, *73*, 227–231.

Hennessy, J. J., and Merrifield, P. R. "A Comparison of the Factor Structures of Mental Abilities in Four Ethnic Groups." *Journal of Educational Psychology*, 1976, *68*, 754–759.

Hills, J. R. "Prediction of College Grades for All Public Colleges for a State." *Journal of Educational Measurement*, 1964, *1*, 155–159.

Humphreys, L. G. "Statistical Definitions of Test Validity for Minority Groups." *Journal of Applied Psychology*, 1973, *58*, 1–4.

Ironson, G. H., and Subkoviak, M. "A Comparison of Several Methods of Assessing Item Bias." *Journal of Educational Measurement*, 1979, *16*, 209–225.

Jackson, G. D. "On the Report of the Ad Hoc Committee on the Educational Uses of Tests with Disadvantaged Students: Another Psychological View from the Association of Black Psychologists." *American Psychologist*, 1975, *30*, 90–93.

Jensen, A. R. "How Biased Are Culture-Loaded Tests?" *Genetic Psychology Monographs,* 1974, *90,* 185–244.

Jensen, A. R. "Test Bias and Construct Validity." *Phi Delta Kappan,* 1976, *59,* 340–346.

Jensen, A. R. "An Examination of Culture Bias on the Wonderlic Personnel Test." *Intelligence,* 1977, *1,* 51–64.

Jensen, A. R. *Bias in Mental Testing.* New York: Free Press, 1980.

Johnson, D. F., and Mihal, W. L. "Performance of Blacks and Whites in Computerized Versus Manual Testing Environments." *American Psychologist,* 1973, *28,* 694–699.

Kallingal, A. "The Prediction of Grades for Black and White Students at Michigan State University." *Journal of Educational Measurement,* 1971, *8,* 263–265.

Katzell, R. A., and Dyer, F. J. "Differential Validity Revived." *Journal of Applied Psychology,* 1977, *62,* 137–145.

Kaufman, A. S. "Factor Analysis of the WISC-R at Eleven Age Levels Between 6½ and 16½ Years." *Journal of Consulting and Clinical Psychology,* 1975, *43,* 135–147.

Linn, R. L. "Fair Test Use in Selection." *Review of Educational Research,* 1973, *43,* 139–161.

Lord, F. M. "A Study of Item Bias Using Item Characteristic Curve Theory." In N. H. Poortinga (Ed.), *Basic Problems in Cross-Cultural Psychology.* Amsterdam: Swits and Vitlinger, 1977.

Lord, F. M. *Applications of Item Response Theory to Practical Testing Problems.* Hillsdale, N.J.: Erlbaum, 1980.

Miele, F. "Cultural Bias in the WISC." *Intelligence,* 1979, *3,* 149–164.

Nungester, R. J. "An Empirical Examination of Three Models of Item Bias." Unpublished doctoral dissertation, Florida State University, 1977.

Pellegrino, J. W., and Glaser, R. "Components of Inductive Reasoning." In R. E. Snow, P. A. Federico, and W. E. Montague (Eds.), *Aptitude, Learning, and Instruction: Cognitive Process Analysis of Aptitude.* Vol. 2. Hillsdale, N.J.: Erlbaum, 1980.

Petersen, N. S. "Bias in the Selection Rule—Bias in the Test." In L. J. T. van der Kamp, W. F. Langerak, and D. N. M. de Gruitjer (Eds.), *Psychometrics for Educational Debates.* London: John Wiley, 1980.

Petersen, N. S., and Novick, M. R. "An Evaluation of Some Models of Culture-Fair Selection." *Journal of Educational Measurement,* 1976, *13,* 3–29.

Pfeifer, C. M., and Sedlacek, W. E. "The Validity of Academic Predictors for Black and White Students at a Predominantly White University." *Journal of Educational Measurement,* 1971, *8,* 253–261.

Pine, S. M. "Reducing Test Bias with Tailored Testing." Paper presented at the International Symposium in Educational Testing, Leyden, June 1977.

Pine, S. M., and Weiss, D. J. *Effects of Item Characteristics on Test Fairness.* Research Report 76-5. Minneapolis: Psychometric Methods Program, University of Minnesota, 1976.

Reschly, D. J. "WISC-R Factor Structures Among Anglos, Blacks, Chicanos, and Native American Papagos." *Journal of Consulting and Clinical Psychology,* 1978, *3,* 417–422.

Reschly, D. J., and Sabers, D. L. "Analysis of Test Bias in Four Groups with the Regression Definition." *Journal of Educational Measurement,* 1979, *16,* 1–9.

Rindler, S. E. "Pitfalls in Assessing Test Speededness." *Journal of Educational Measurement,* 1979, *16,* 261–270.

Rock, D. A., and Werts, C. E. *Construct Validity of the SAT Across Populations: An Empirical Confirmatory Study.* Princeton, N.J.: Educational Testing Service, 1979.

Rock, D. A., Werts, C. E., and Grandy, J. *Construct Validity of the GRE Across Populations: An Empirical Confirmatory Study.* Princeton, N.J.: Educational Testing Service, 1980.

Rudner, L. M. "An Evaluation of Select Approaches for Biased Item Identification." Unpublished doctoral dissertation, Catholic University of America, 1977.

Rudner, L. M., Getson, P. R., and Knight, D. L. "Biased Item Detection Techniques." *Journal of Educational Statistics,* 1980a, *5,* 213–233.

Rudner, L. M., Getson, P. R., and Knight, D. L. "A Monte Carlo Comparison of Seven Biased Item Detection Techniques." *Journal of Educational Measurement,* 1980b, *17,* 1–10.

Scheuneman, J. "A New Method of Assessing Bias in Test Items." Paper presented at the annual meeting of the American Educational Research Association, Washington, D.C., April 1975.

Scheuneman, J. "Ethnic Group Bias in Intelligence Test Items." In S. W. Lundsteen (Ed.), *Cultural Factors in Learning and Instruction.* Diversity Series, No. 56. New York: ERIC Clearinghouse on Urban Education, 1978.

Scheuneman, J. "A Method of Assessing Bias in Test Items." *Journal of Educational Measurement,* 1979, *16,* 143–152.

Scheuneman, J. "A Posteriori Analysis of Biased Items." In R. A. Berk (Ed.), *Handbook of Methods for Detecting Test Bias.* Baltimore, Md.: Johns Hopkins University Press, in press.

Schmidt, F. L., and Crano, W. D. "A Test of the Theory of Fluid and Crystallized Intelligence in Middle- and Low-Socioeconomic-Status Children." *Journal of Educational Psychology,* 1974, *66,* 255–261.

Schmidt, F. L., and Hunter, J. E. "Racial and Ethnic Bias in Psychological Tests: Divergent Implications of Two Definitions of Test Bias." *American Psychologist,* 1974, *29,* 1–8.

Shepard, L. A. "Definitions of Bias." In R. A. Berk (Ed.), *Handbook of Methods for Detecting Test Bias.* Baltimore, Md.: Johns Hopkins University Press, in press.

Shepard, L., Camilli, G., and Averill, M. "Comparison of Six Procedures for Detecting Test Item Bias Using Both Internal and External Ability Criteria." *Journal of Educational Statistics,* 1981, *6,* 317–375.

Silverman, B. I., Barton, F., and Lyon, M. "Minority Group Status and Bias in College Admissions Criteria." *Educational and Psychological Measurement,* 1976, *36,* 401–407.

Sinnott, L. T. *Differences in Item Performance Across Groups.* Princeton, N.J.: Educational Testing Service, 1980.

Skanes, G. R., Sullivan, A. M., Rowe, E. J., and Shannon, E. "Intelligence and Transfer: Aptitude by Treatment Interactions." *Journal of Educational Psychology,* 1974, *66,* 563–568.

Snow, R. E. "Aptitude Processes." In R. E. Snow, P. A. Federico, and W. E. Montague (Eds.), *Aptitude, Learning, and Instruction: Cognitive Process Analysis of Aptitude.* Vol. 2. Hillsdale, N.J.: Erlbaum, 1980.

Stanley, J. C., and Porter, A. C. "Correlations of Scholastic Aptitude Test Scores with College Grades for Negroes Versus Whites." *Journal of Educational Measurement,* 1967, *4,* 199–218.

Sternberg, R. "Component Processes in Analogical Reasoning." *Psychological Review,* 1977, *89,* 353–378.

Stricker, L. J. *A New Index of Differential Subgroup Performance: Application to the GRE Aptitude Test.* Princeton, N.J.: Educational Testing Service, 1981.

Swinton, S. S. *Predictive Bias in Graduate Admissions Test.* Princeton, N.J.: Educational Testing Service, 1981.

Temp, G. "Test Bias: Validity of the SAT for Blacks and Whites in Thirteen Integrated Institutions." *Journal of Educational Measurement,* 1971, *8,* 245–251.

Thorndike, R. L. "Concepts of Culture Fairness." *Journal of Educational Measurement,* 1971a, *8,* 63–70.

Thorndike, R. L. "Memorandum on the Use of the Lorge-Thorndike Tests in California." Unpublished manuscript, February 26, 1971b.

Weitzman, R. A. *Test Bias and Overprediction.* Monterey, Calif.: Naval Postgraduate School, 1979.

Whitely, S. E. "Solving Verbal Analogies: Some Cognitive Components of Intelligence Test Items." *Journal of Educational Psychology,* 1976, *6,* 232–242.

Whitely, S. E., and Dawis, R. V. "Effects of Cognitive Intervention on Latent Ability Measured from Analogy Items." *Journal of Educational Psychology,* 1974, *66,* 710–717.

Wightman, L. E. "Study of LSAT Item Performance for Different Subgroups." Unpublished manuscript, October 1979.

Williams, R. L., Mosby, D., and Hinson, V. "Critical Issues in Achievement Testing of Children from Diverse Ethnic Backgrounds." In M. J. Wargo and D. R. Green (Eds.), *Achievement Testing of Disadvantaged and Minority Students for Educational Program Evaluation.* Monterey, Calif.: CTB/McGraw-Hill, 1978.

Janice Dowd Scheuneman is director of statistical analysis, elementary and secondary school programs, Educational Testing Service, Princeton, New Jersey.

The interpretation of commonly used, individually administered abilities
tests relies on largely unvalidated clinical inferences and judgments.
This chapter discusses the limitations of some widely used intelligence
tests and describes three emerging models of assessment.

Clinical and Diagnostic Assessment of Children's Abilities: Traditional and Innovative Models

James J. Hennessy

At some point in his or her school experience, virtually every child in this country is exposed to tests of mental abilities. These tests may be measures of a multitude of abilities or aptitudes, such as the Differential Aptitude Tests (DAT) or the Primary Mental Abilities Test (PMAT); they may be measures of scholastic aptitude, such as the Short Form Test of Academic Aptitude (SFTAA) or the Academic Promise Test (APT); or they may be measures of general ability, such as the Lorge-Thorndike Intelligence Tests or the California Test of Mental Maturity (CTMM).

The information derived from these measures is used for a wide variety of purposes. These purposes include grouping for instruction, selection for special programs, guidance and counseling for vocational and academic planning, and evaluation of the effects of instruction. Sometimes, the data are merely recorded in permanent files and not used at all. To a large extent, however, data gathered from group-administered tests of ability are considered too imprecise for decision making about the children who are experiencing difficulties in school. When circumstances that dictate the need for a more accurate assessment arise, individually administered tests are used. The most frequently used measures are the Stanford-Binet, or one of the Wechsler scales: Wechsler

P. Merrifield (Ed.). *New Directions for Testing and Measurement: Measuring Human Abilities*, no. 12.
San Francisco: Jossey-Bass, December 1981.

Preschool and Primary Scale of Intelligence (WPPSI), the Wechsler Intelligence Scale for Children, Revised (WISC-R), or the Wechsler Adult Intelligence Scale, Revised (WAIS-R).

In this chapter, the uses of individually administered abilities tests in schools will be explored. Then, some of the new directions in which abilities assessment may go will be considered. Before we examine current practice and future trends, however, it may be helpful to view intelligence testing from a historical perspective.

Theory and Practice Diverge

Psychometric theory and assessment trace their origins to late nineteenth-century England and France. In England, Galton and his associates were attempting to find the correlates of successful achievement. Guided by Darwinian theory, they gathered extensive measurements of sensory, motor, and physical characteristics, including head size, in the belief that intelligent performance depended on the biological makeup of the individual. To go beyond sensory-physical data, tests of increasingly more complex "mental" functioning were also developed. By the early twentieth century, investigators were no longer as concerned with assessment of physical correlates of intelligence, but the statistical methodologies developed by Galton to measure strength of relationships between measures were adopted as the foundation stones of individual difference theory and research.

Spearman (1927), whose major work is summarized in *The Abilities of Man,* was among the first to formulate a scientific theory of complex intellectual functioning from a cognitive point of view. Wundt and his colleagues at Leipzig had developed substantial theory and a large amount of data on sensations through the techniques of introspection and complication experiments using reaction time as the dependent measure. Wundt concluded that higher-level mental processes could not be assessed by his chosen techniques. Ebbinghaus made a significant breakthrough in the analysis of memory, defined in modern terms as rote and short-term. So it remained for Galton, who had pioneered the development of the questionnaire, to focus on higher-level mental processes that were available for inspection by an external observer. Spearman applied this approach to the assessment of school learning and the individual differences in achievement that were apparent even among the highly selected students in the public schools of that era. (The selection, it should be noted, took place on the basis of social class. Then, as now, differences in intelligence among persons within a socially defined stratum were much larger than differences between means of persons in different strata.) This research was guided only to a limited extent by practical concerns, such as diagnosis or prediction of school achievement; rather, Spearman and his coworkers were more interested in understanding the structure and nature of higher mental functioning.

Contemporaneously with the works of early British investigators, Binet, an experimental psychologist, and his colleagues also took an interest in the assessment of intellectual functioning, but for reasons that were more pragmatic than Spearman's. Their concern was to develop an objective procedure for identifying intellectually defective children, that is, children who were likely to have difficulty mastering the curriculum of Parisian schools. Binet rejected the earlier British emphasis on sensory functioning as an indicator of intellectual acuity and emphasized the role of memory, reasoning, and judgment as the higher processes that contributed most to predictions of individual differences in ability. The focus of this work, which was guided by Binet's beliefs about the organization and structure of intellectual functioning, was more applied than theoretical.

The Binet-Simon scale, originally published in 1905 and revised in 1908 and again in 1911, represented the first attempt to quantify the concept *intelligence* (Brody and Brody, 1976). The scale included tests of ten processes believed to represent the several intellectual faculties. The anomaly evident in the scale is that, although Binet viewed intelligence as comprised of diverse sets of independent abilities or faculties, he pioneered the development of a single-score index to represent these complex abilities. His own work reflects the split between the theory and practice then current, where theory viewed intelligence as a complex multifaceted construct and practice required a single index useful in guiding and directing educational decision making. This tendency to consider intelligence as a single entity was enhanced by Stern's definition of IQ as the ratio of mental age to chronological age.

The impact of Binet's work was felt quickly in the United States. By 1916, Terman had published an adapted version of the Binet-Simon scale, the now widely used Stanford-Binet. In this country, the new instrument was used primarily for assessment purposes. Only occasionally was there concern for greater understanding of the construct intelligence. The value of the then-new index of ability was recognized during World War I, which brought with it the need for a brief, objectively scored scale that could be used to determine fitness for military training. The works of Otis and his associates led to development of the first standardized group test that yielded an index of intellectual ability. By the beginning of the second decade of this century, intelligence testing was widely practiced in schools, by the military, and for immigration screening, in an attempt to detect intellectually subnormal individuals. It should be noted that this use of an instrument heavily loaded with language ability led to great misunderstandings about the intelligence of certain ethnic groups, particularly that of middle Europeans, and that these unwarranted stereotypes were not defused until a generation or two later.

It was not until well after applied uses were firmly in place that researchers in this country began systematic studies to determine the nature and structure of intelligence and that the validity of available tests as measures of intelligence was questioned. As perhaps in other fields, the needs of society for technological advances outstripped the development of theory. As Sattler (1974) pointed out in his history of the Stanford-Binet, that scale helped to establish the field of clinical psychology, and it brought intelligence testing into many institutions, most particularly the schools. However, "the intelligence testing movement developed without the backing of any particular school or system, and it grew because of practical demands (Sattler, 1974, p. 95). Although it is possible that Binet himself would not have agreed that the intelligence quotient derived by others from his scale did in fact represent a measure of global intelligence, the Stanford-Binet IQ soon became almost synonymous with intelligence and all that that term conveys. Thus, an index originally devised to identify school potential was reified by many psychologists and educators and by most of the public as a quality possessed by all people but to differing degrees. This new discriminator developed in the almost complete absence of sound psychological theory. Even so, it was accepted as the standard against which later measures of mental ability were to be validated.

It is not surprising, then, to find that present-day assessment practice is still heavily influenced by an atheoretical, clinical, pragmatic standard. This point was emphasized by Brody and Brody (1976) in their discussion of the use of intelligence tests in clinical practice today. Commenting on the many suggestions given in widely used clinical texts for interpretation of test profiles and patterns, they stated: "the inferences and interpretations drawn from various observations of behavior in test situations, responses to items, and patterns of subtest scores are rarely, if ever, supported by appeal to relevant empirical evidence. Rather, such inferences are presented to the neophyte psychologist ex cathedra as the result of the accumulated wisdom of the practicing psychologist. And, indeed, it is not unknown for such inferences to be taught to psychologists even where the accumulated evidence has shown them to be incorrect" (Brody and Brody, 1976, p. 22). As will be demonstrated in this chapter, clinical use and empirical evidence are still not in harmony.

Wechsler's Contributions

The major impetus for the detailed clinical use of intelligence tests was Wechsler's development of a multiscale instrument, the Wechsler-Bellevue Scale, and its subsequent extensions and revisions. The original scale was developed partly in response to criticisms of the shortcomings of the Stanford-Binet. Three such criticisms were that the Stanford-Binet's age-related scoring system rendered the scale difficult to interpret for adults, that the similarity of tasks tended to favor verbally able individuals at the older age levels, and that the Stanford-Binet's single score did not provide sufficient diagnostic information. Wechsler developed a scale that tapped several different abilities and at the same time yielded an accurate measure of general intelligence. His definition of intelligence as an "aggregate global capacity . . . to act purposefully, to think rationally, and to deal effectively with [the] environment" (Matarazzo,

1972, p. 79) guided scale construction. He included tests that although not pure measures of primary mental abilities in Thurstone's sense, did ultimately measure global ability in aggregate. Wechsler recognized quite clearly that functional intelligence was more than the sum of scores on the subtests of his scale, yet he stated that "the IQ remains a basic concept in the measurement of intelligence and, indeed, as unequivocal a definition of the currently testable aspect of intellectual functioning as is probable" (Matarazzo, 1972, p. 101).

From an assessment perspective, the major difference between Terman and Wechsler lies in the amount and diversity of information yielded by the Wechsler scales. The currently available Wechsler scales yield at least fourteen scores. The WISC-R has six verbal subtests, which are summed to obtain a verbal IQ; six performance tests, which yield a performance IQ; and a full-scale IQ obtained from a composite of verbal and performance scores. The WPPSI and WAIS-R have eleven subtests and yield the three IQ scores just mentioned. The rich data obtained from these scales led to the development of many procedures and recommendations for the interpretation of score differences, configurations, and clusters as indicators of or contributors to a host of problems confronting the psychologist. The diagnostic value of the scales came to have greater meaning than the aggregate IQ score. As already mentioned, not all psychologists agree that the scales are valid for many of these uses.

As this brief review of the origins of individual testing of ability indicates, the use of such scales in schools and other settings is intended primarily to provide information about individuals so that the problems affecting them can be better understood. Clinical judgment and experience, rather than theory based on empirical evidence, have guided use and interpretation. Although psychometrists have developed elaborate theories of intelligence during the past fifty years, the findings and instruments developed through their efforts have been overshadowed by clinical assessment.

Current Uses of Intelligence Tests

Information about an individual derived from individually administered tests is part of a complete psychological assessment, which is seen as distinct from a psychometric evaluation. "Psychometric testing attempts to describe and measure differences among many individuals along presumed psychological traits. In psychological assessment, however, an attempt is made to assess some particular problem involving one specific individual" (Maloney and Ward, 1976, p. 39). Most often, a complete assessment includes test scores, interview, observation, and biographical data. The scores are seen as only one source of data, not as the complete process or end point of assessment.

Although most textbooks and manuals on psychological assessment emphasize the limited capabilities of intelligence tests, these measures are still a major part of the assessment process. Their use, therefore, ought to rest on evidence that important psychological characteristics underlie or are related to the test and that differences among people on the test relate to differences in performance on some meaningful nontest behavior. Basically, it is assumed that every interpretation of an individual's performance on a test is supported by evidence of a relationship between the test and some criterion behavior or construct. The validity of tests used for individual assessment must be demonstrated for the specific use of the measure, as no test is inherently valid, and as we shall see, construct validity is generally the most important concern.

What, then, are the purposes of testing? According to Cronbach (1971), there are two basic purposes: to obtain information that can be used in making decisions about a person, and to obtain information that describes a person. The first basic purpose includes testing for selection, placement, and evaluation. Each of these three uses provides experts or institutions with data which influence decisions that have to be made about individuals.

The use of tests for selection, although widespread in colleges, universities, and business, is limited in school because public schools must admit virtually all students. Probably the only times when individually administered tests are used for selection purposes are in connection with admission to programs for the gifted and talented or for specialized vocational training. For students already in school, placement in appropriate instructional groups is usually accomplished with data from group-administered tests. For placement decisions in special classes or in programs for the mentally retarded and learning handicapped, individually administered tests are used almost exclusively.

The primary use of individually administered tests in schools today is to obtain descriptions of functioning for the purpose of diagnosis of children thought to be learning disabled, neurologically impaired, developmentally disabled, or emotionally disturbed. In the regulations of many states — and in the *Diagnostic and Statistical Manual* of the American Psychiatric Association (American Psychiatric Association, 1980) — it is specified that individually administered abilities measures shall be included as part of the diagnosis of children prior to classification or assignment to special educational programs. Because the diagnostic use of tests is so prevalent today, an analysis of their validities will be presented later in this chapter.

Regardless of the specific reasons for testing, the conscientious interpreter of scores will require evidence of appropriate validity. When tests are used for selection and placement, evidence of criterion validity is often sufficient. Criterion validity implies that the brief samples of behavior represented by the test are correlated with relevant nontest behavior. As such, the concern is not so much with what the tests measure as it is with how well they predict it. Empirical evidence of the magnitude of these relations determines the suitability of a given test for this purpose. There exists a substantial body of literature supporting the criterion validity of ability tests (Buros, 1978).

If, however, a test is used to describe, diagnose, or determine the psychological traits, factors, or characteristics that underlie behavior, then evidence of construct validity is generally required. Because one of the goals of diagnostic assessment is to uncover either the etiological or contributing factors of a problem, interpretations are often made about the effects of relatively stable underlying traits and their effects on behavior. Inferences about underlying traits require construct validity in the particular instance, for, as Cronbach said (1971, p. 447), "One validates not a test but an *interpretation of the data arising from a specified procedure* . . . . because every interpretation has its own degree of validity, one can never reach the simple conclusion that a particular test 'is valid.'"

While it has long been recognized that validity is a highly specific characteristic, much clinical assessment proceeds from less than firmly anchored evidence. For example, in discussing the validity of the WAIS, Anastasi (1976, p. 252) commented that Wechsler's manuals and books treat validity "essentially in terms of content validity, although [they have] overtones of construct validity without supporting data. Much of the discussion . . . [deals] with the construct global intelligence but [has] only a tenuous relation to the evaluation of the WAIS as a measuring instrument" for most clinical applications. As later sections of this chapter will show, similar comments can be made about other scales widely used in school settings.

A critical assumption in diagnostic assessment requiring evidence of construct validity is that the scales "are accurate enough to identify deficits and [that] low scores represent low areas of functioning" (Lidz, 1981, p. 9). Although interpretation of high scores based on content validity may be safe at times, the same cannot be said of low scores, "since low scores . . . may reflect quantitatively different processes from the skills indicative of high scores— such as inattention, anxiety, defensiveness, low maturation, or illness— constuct validity is . . . critical" (Messick, 1979, p. 284). Two important questions must be considered in evaluating present practice in the assessment of mental abilities. First, do the tests and their components adequately tap or explain differences in performance in terms of meaningful underlying psychological dimensions? Second, are the types of interpretations that many users make warranted by the supporting data?

Adequacy of Available Tests for Diagnosis

In this section, we shall review some recent research on assessment to determine whether there are measures that provide evidence which addresses these two questions. The most frequent use of abilities measures in schools today is to diagnose the learning problems subsumed under the term *learning disabilities*. Controversy and confusion abound in the literature about the definition of this term, so we shall not attempt to define it here. It will suffice to say that the learning disabilities label is applied only after many other possibilities for explaining low or diminished academic achievement, such as retardation, emotional problems, environmental deprivation, or physical impairment, have been discounted. Since it is a catchall category, it is not surprising that there are many conflicting "theories" to explain it and a large number of scales that purport to diagnose it.

The most recent *Mental Measurement Yearbook* (Buros, 1978) indicates that there are at least twenty-nine published individually administered tests of general ability available to users and at least forty-five individually administered tests of specific abilities and learning disabilities. If the number of published studies is a valid indicator of the acceptance for particular tests, then the Wechsler scales and the Stanford-Binet must be viewed as the most popular abilities measures. As of 1977, the last year in which the literature was reviewed, the *Mental Measurement Yearbook* (Buros, 1978) cited 1,590 articles for the Stanford-Binet since its publication in 1916 and 1,585 for the WISC and WISC-R and 1,291 for the WAIS since their publication in the late 1940s. In the area of specific abilities and learning disabilities, the Illinois Test of Psycholinguistic Abilities (ITPA) is among the leaders in use, with more than 640 citations since its publication. While it is not possible to review and summarize all these studies, we shall only consider studies that provide evidence of differential diagnostic validity.

Specific Abilities Measures

Recently, Coles (1978) and Arter and Jenkins (1979) have reviewed the literature on the validity of the most frequently used individually administered measures of specific abilities. Tests of psycholinguistic abilities, such as the Illinois Test of Psycholinguistic Abilities, of visual perception, such as the Bender Visual-Motor Gestalt Test and the Frostig Developmental Test of Visual Perception, and of auditory perception, such as the Wepman Auditory Discrimination Test, were reviewed in these studies to assess their predictive, diagnostic, and construct validities. Both reviews point to serious deficiencies in presently used tests.

Arter and Jenkins (1979) reviewed evidence of concurrent, predictive, diagnostic, and construct validities. The findings regarding the ITPA are illustrative of their major conclusions regarding the tests that they cited. Evidence of concurrent validity, of predictive validity, or of correlation between the ITPA and other tests given at the same time was generally not found. Only three subtests (Grammatic Closure, Sound Blending, and Auditory Association) and total score consistently had moderate ($r > .35$) correlations with reading achievement tests. When IQ was controlled, only Grammatic Closure and total score had satisfactory correlations with achievement. Arter and Jenkins concluded that "It is difficult to escape the general conclusion that measurement devices traditionally used in differential diagnosis lack concurrent criterion validity with respect to academic skills" (1979, p. 529). The findings regarding the ability of these measures to predict later achievement were similar to the findings for concurrent validity. Because so few studies of predictive validity involve an interval of more than one year, firm conclusions about these measures must await additional longitudinal evidence. Arter and Jenkins defined diagnostic validity as the ability of a test to differentiate between groups of good and poor readers, because prediction of reading performance is the most frequent and important use of these measures. Evidence for diagnostic validity was virtually nonexistent for the ITPA and other measures, except for some auditory perception tests. Citing earlier reviews, Arter and Jenkins found that no ITPA subtest was able to differentiate groups of good and poor readers with any consistency across different situations; it seemed possible, however, that in every situation, some combination of subtests could be put together to predict reading performance group membership. Since most investigators of ITPA and similar specific abilities tests do not report whether differences in intelligence were controlled for, it is difficult to determine whether success rates would remain as high if investigators were to control for such differences.

The measures of specific abilities are also suspect as measures of meaningful constructs separate from general intelligence. Factor analytic studies summarized by Arter and Jenkins (1979, p. 537) indicate that the ITPA appears to be "a measure of cognitive functioning or intelligence rather than of perceptual or psycholinguistic abilities." No evidence was cited to support the construct validity of the subtests as measures of specific abilities. The problems with the ITPA led one reviewer to state that "This test should not have been published, at least in its present form" (Lumsden, 1978, p. 578) and another to caution, "It would be unfortunate if the ITPA were to be used to diagnose or categorize children as having 'language,' 'psycholinguistic,' or 'learning disabilities' problems and/or as a basis for planning remedial programs" (Weiderholt, 1978, p. 582). Similarly disappointing results and conclusions were cited by Coles (1978), who went so far as to predict that most, if not all, of the tests that he reviewed could eventually be discarded in favor of new models of dysfunction and new assessment procedures. Given that a major weakness of most individually administered diagnostic tests is their substantial correlation with general intelligence, it is necessary to examine general ability measures using the validity criteria cited earlier for specific abilities.

General Ability Measures

The Stanford-Binet and the Wechsler scales dominate the field of individual assessment. Evidence bearing on their concurrent, predictive, and construct validities is plentiful. Literally thousands of studies supporting these scales have appeared in the literature since 1916. IQ as measured by these tests is reported to correlate significantly with performance in school, college, and jobs and is probably the best predictor of achievement available to psychologists, according to Jensen (1980). Indeed, the correlation between intelligence test scores and academic performance is "so generally consistent and statistically uncontestable . . . that even the harshest critics of mental testing wholly concede the substantial relationship between IQ and scholastic achievement" (Jensen, 1980, p. 316).

When it is used for differential diagnosis of school-related problems, however, the evidence for its validity is less compelling. The WISC and WISC-R, rather than the Stanford-Binet, are used for differential diagnosis because of the scores available on the subtests. The most common practice is to analyze the scatter or spread of scores on the subtests, which have standardized means of ten and standard deviations of three points, and composite indices. According to Sattler (1974), differences between the verbal and performance scores, between a subtest and another subtest, between a subtest and an average of other subtests, or between a subtest and verbal performance or full-scale scores form the basis of scatter, pattern, or profile analysis. An individual's profile of performance on the scales is compared with profiles of previously identified diagnostic groups to formulate hypotheses about the person's dysfunction. The profile can also be used to assess an individual's relative strengths and weaknesses.

The manual (Wechsler, 1974) and clinical texts (such as, Sattler, 1974) suggest that differences of three or more points between subtest scores can be significant and have interpretive or diagnostic value. A fifteen-point difference between verbal and performance scores is also considered significant. These guidelines were developed after confidence intervals were calculated for each of the WISC-R scores, using standard errors of measurement. If two intervals for a given level of confidence do not overlap (for example, the 15 percent level recommended by Wechsler, 1974), they are considered to be assessing reliable different performance. The confidence level is defined as the range, centered on an obtained scale score for a person, within which the true score for that person on that scale is expected to be, with a specified confidence that that expectation could be realized (by estimating the true score as the limit of converging averages of repeated observations of that person on that scale, were it feasible so to test); the 95 percent confidence interval, for example, is the range, centered on an obtained score, and extending in both directions for 1.96 standard errors of measurement, a unit based on the standard deviation of the obtained scores and the reliability of the scoring,procedure. The greater the reliability the narrower the confidence interval for expected values of true score.

Overlap is said to be worthy of consideration if the upper bound of a confidence interval for true score on one subscale is greater than the lower 15 percent of the values of the true score expected for the same person if he gets a higher obtained score on another subscale; these values, in turn, are based on that person's obtained score, the standard deviation and the reliability of the second subscale. If the person gets a lower score on the second subscale, overlap is said to occur if the lower bound of the confidence interval for the first subscale is less than the higher 15 percent of expected true score values on the second subscale. In either case, the less the reliability of either or both obtained scores, the greater the possibility of overlap with regard to true scores. What is not clearly pointed out is that reliability and validity are not synonymous. Unless there is evidence that the tests being compared assess different abilities, differences in scores on two tests may be a function of equally reliable but different methods of assessing the same ability (for example, the recall of specific facts on the Information and Vocabulary subtests). The manual and many texts confuse standard errors of measurement with standard errors of estimate when they base diagnostic statements on reliability data rather than on validity data.

This point was demonstrated quite explicitly by Kaufman (1976), one of the authors of the WISC-R. He analyzed the data gathered during standardization of the WISC-R to determine the amount of spread between highest and lowest subtest scores found in this large, representative group (n = 2,200). He calculated the absolute scale-score difference between the highest and lowest subtest scores for each child in the standardization group. Means and standard deviations of these difference scores were computed for the entire sample and for each of the eleven age groups for which norms were developed. The magnitude of the mean high-low differences on the subtests was surprisingly large. For the entire group, the mean point difference was 7, with a standard deviation of $\pm$ 2. The mean differences for the eleven age groups (six-and-a-half to sixteen) ranged from 6.7 to 7.3, with $\pm$ 1.9 and 2.3 deviation units. Variability was greatest for the high full-scale groups (IQs above 120). The amount of spread evidenced led Kaufman to warn that clinical or diagnostic users should "keep in mind that it is common for [large] differences to be seen" (1976, p. 164). He suggested that most clinicians may have a "flat-profile stereotype" of "normal" youngsters, who may be thought to perform at the same level on all the subtests, since so few "normal" youngsters are seen in practice. Most clinicians may not be aware of the marked variation in scores within profiles exhibited by "normal" children. The manual certainly does not provide this information. Diagnostic inferences cannot be made safely if the scatter found fits "normal" profiles. While three-point differences may be reliable, they probably do not reflect significant departures from normality, statistically and clinically speaking.

The meaning of a verbal performance difference of fifteen points or greater is also not clear. In the clinical literature, Matarazzo (1972), Sattler (1974), and Coles (1978) give importance to the fact that the data analyzed by Kaufman and reported in the manual, suggest that differences that large occurred frequently in the standardization group. Differences of fifteen points were found in approximately 25 percent of the profiles, and differences as large as twenty points occurred in more than 10 percent of the profiles. Although users may be reasonably certain of the reliability of the subtests and of the difference in scores between them, they should realize that such differences may be more "normal" than unusual.

In doing profile analysis, one also assumes that the subtests are valid measures of specific underlying abilities. Factor analytic studies reviewed by Sattler (1974) generally found a verbal comprehension and performance factor supporting interpretation of the verbal and performance IQ scores. The validity of using interpretations of selected subtests as indicators of underlying abilities has received only mixed support. Kaufman's analyses of the data derived during standardization do not provide firm support for such use (Kaufman, 1975). His data indicate that all the subtests are heavily loaded by a general factor. The first unrotated principal factors extracted for each of the eleven age groups accounted for between 79 percent and 92 percent of common factor variance. Rotations to orthogonal solutions were computed after applying several criteria for determining the number of factors that adequately represented the WISC-R. Two-factor solutions met the criteria for six of the age groups, while a third factor emerged for five of the groups. The first two factors in all the solutions closely represented the verbal and performance partition originally developed by Wechsler. The third factor was similar to a Freedom from Distractability factor found in several earlier factor analyses of the WISC. The orthogonal factor structures were seen by Kaufman as evidence of the validity of the verbal and performance IQ scores.

However, the oblique rotations reported by Kaufman do not clearly support that conclusion. Those analyses indicated that the median correlation between the verbal and performance factors, using Oblimax procedures, was .65; the median correlation of those two factors with the Freedom from Distractability factor was .47. These results suggest that there is a strong second-order factor underlying the WISC-R. Thus, the notion that independent verbal and performance estimates can be derived from the WISC-R is not supported.

Kaufman then looked at the amount of specific variance associated with each subtest at each age level. Specific variance is obtained by calculating the difference between the communality of a test and its reliability. He suggested that a subtest had interpretable differential meaning if the percent of specific variance exceeded the percent of error variance, an admittedly arbitrary criterion. All but three subtests (Vocabulary, Comprehension, and Object Assembly) had more specific variance than error variance; none of the subtests had more specific variance than common factor variance; and the subtests with the highest proportion of specific variance (Digit Span, Picture Arrangement, and Coding) are among the least reliable (Wechsler, 1974). The interpretive value of these three subtests is restricted by their low reliability. The relatively low proportions of specific variance found for the other subtests and the presence of a general factor accounting for approximately 80 percent of the common factor variance do not provide support for the practice of interpreting WISC-R subtests as measures of specific abilities. The results suggest that Wechsler's original intent to develop a scale that estimates intelligence in aggregate has been successful, but there is little evidence of the WISC-R's empirical validity beyond that use.

Future Directions in Ability Assessment

As already indicated, present abilities assessment and diagnosis procedures generally do not provide sufficient information on which to base treatment decisions. Most of the widely used measures are highly correlated with
general or global intelligence, so they cannot offer information about specific
deficits or strengths. Several alternative assessment procedures have been
reported recently that may correct inadequacies in existing practice. These
new models are Learning Potential Assessment (LPA), Neuropsychological
Assessment (NPA), and Multicomponent Latent Trait Analysis (MCLTA).
The areas of concern of the three models are somewhat different, but they all
undertake to explain and diagnose individual differences in learning. LPA attempts to assess and then to compensate for environmental factors that influence performance on tests. NPA looks for differences or deficits in specific
brain functioning to explain differences in ability and achievement, while
MCLTA analyzes both task and learner characteristics to predict or possibly
diagnose achievement difficulties. Each model will be discussed here, and
where it is available, empirical evidence will be explored.

Learning Potential Assessment. A major issue in the diagnosis of mental and educational retardation is the extent to which psychometric test performance is influenced by prior experience and environment. Mercer (1978),
Jensen (1980), and Budoff (1975) all provide evidence of the strong relationship between socioeconomic status and IQ. These findings have led Budoff
and others to suggest that IQ represents only one aspect of intelligence and
that sociocultural factors and previous learning experiences must be accounted
for in order to estimate learning potential accurately.

Over the past ten years, many school districts and cities and some
states have discontinued wide-scale IQ testing because of apparent IQ test
bias. Courts in several states have also ordered IQ tests not to be used for decisions about special class placements if such tests identify a disproportionate
number of minority children as mentally retarded. Court and legislative decisions have not always been rooted in clear evidence of psychometrically determined bias; sometimes, they have been based on apparent unfair use of test
results (Jensen, 1980). The issues and controversies surrounding use of such
tests with minority and deprived children are beyond the scope of this chapter.
Rather, we will look at some procedures developed recently to yield more
accurate ability assessment.

In her study of the mentally retarded, Mercer (1973) found that a disproportionate number of disadvantaged and minority school-age chldren were
diagnosed as mentally retarded on the basis of IQ test performance. Many of
these children, however, were found to be able to function quite adequately in
the home and community, and they were not deficient in social skills or other
adaptive behaviors. Mercer claimed that these children were situationally
retarded and that, when such background factors as membership in a minority
sociocultural group were controlled, differences in test performance between

majority and minority children decreased substantially. She developed a new assessment procedure, the System of Multicultural Pluralistic Assessment (SOMPA) (Mercer, 1978), which corrected the psychometric IQ obtained from the WISC-R by adding in a value computed from her complex Adaptive Behavior Inventory for Children (ABIC).

The ABIC assesses a child's functioning in five social systems—family, community, peer group, school, and career/consumer—through interviews with parents. Assessment of these domains provides an estimate of the child's ability to function outside school. Norms for various subcultural groups have been developed, and procedures for adjusting psychometrically tested IQ are now available (Mercer, 1978). According to Mercer, SOMPA should allow for more accurate assessment of ability, and it should decrease the disproportionate number of minority youngsters identified as EMR (Educable Mentally Retarded). As yet, there is insufficient evidence of SOMPA's validity.

The focus of learning potential assessment as proposed by Budoff (1975) and Feuerstein (1979) is not to determine what a child knows at the time of initial testing but rather to assess how well the child can learn after exposure to and training on tasks similar to those in the test. The model assumes that many youngsters diagnosed as educationally retarded have not had prior experience with the types of tasks included on such tests as the WISC-R and the Stanford-Binet. This lack of previous experience is found most frequently among the disadvantaged and minorities.

The LPA models operate on the hypothesis that training children on tasks similar to those used on tests and then assessing the subsequent improvement in their performance provides an effective means of reducing the effects of initial differences in performance. The posttraining test score provides a more accurate measure of learning potential. Basically, Budoff's model is a test-teach-retest one, in which systematic instruction is given. He typically uses matrix completion problems like those in the Raven's Progressive Matrices (RPM). The RPM is viewed as a good measure of intelligence (Jensen, 1980), and it measures conceptual ability, analogical reasoning, and capacity to form comparisons, all of which are related to Binet's and Wechsler's conceptions of intelligence.

The LPA model challenges the assumption that intelligence cannot be taught and that coaching has no effect on abilities test performance. Both Budoff and Feuerstein hold that, if a child has ability but if experience has not allowed that ability to be expressed, then systematic training will uncover it. In effect, it is possible to diagnose those who are actually deficient in ability from those who were never taught how to develop that ability.

Research findings to date have been inconsistent. Budoff (1975) reports substantial gains in posttest performance on the RPM for disadvantaged EMR children exposed to training as compared with controls who were similar but received no training. He also found that lower-functioning children made significantly greater gains than average-functioning children. He interpreted these findings as supportive of his "accounting for lack of experience" hypothesis. According to him, middle- and upper-class children of average and above-average ability function at their optimum or maximum levels of mental testing and thus do not show gains after instruction.

Popoff-Warner (1980) tested these claims by studying thirty EMR and thirty non-EMR youngsters from several socioeconomic levels. Youngsters were assigned to a training group, to a practice control group, or to a "pure" control group as the result of their performance on the RPM. These sixty scores were ranked from high to low. The three children with the highest scores formed the first of twenty blocks. Each block member was randomly assigned to one of the three groups. The procedure was repeated for each subsequent block of three students until all students had been assigned to a group. Training followed Budoff's procedures of systematic exposure to tasks, while the practice control group simply took two tests similar to the RPM with no instruction, and the control group took only the pre- and posttests on the RPM.

Popoff-Warner's results were not fully consistent with LPA hypotheses. Children in the training group had significantly higher posttest scores on the RPM. There was not, however, greater gain for EMR youngsters, as the model predicted. Moreover, the posttest scores of the EMR youngsters in the training group did not approach the pretest mean of the non-EMR group, as had been hypothesized. Surprisingly, the practice-only control group also showed significant improvement and did not differ significantly from the training group on the posttest. Only the EMR "pure" control group showed no significant pre-post differences. Socioeconomic status did not interact with ability to affect posttest improvement in all groups. Disadvantaged low-functioning children, regardless of group assignment, exhibited the greatest overall gain. These findings were interpreted as support for the effects of training and practice on test performance but not for the major assumptions about inaccuracies in the assessment of children of lower socioeconomic status and lower ability.

One may generalize from the available literature that performance on a second assessment will be higher than on the first if some training or practice is given. There are no data, however, to indicate whether second assessment scores predict performance in school better than the original scores do. There also are no data to indicate whether the skills taught to enhance test performance transfer to important nontest tasks involved in mastering basic academic skills. If such transfer of training cannot be demonstrated, LPA will not contribute greatly to assessment. Long ago, Jensen (1969) suggested that increasing scores on IQ tests was not a sufficient or ultimate goal of intervention. The appropriate goal was to enhance academic achievement. The proponents of LPA have yet to demonstrate its validity in this area.

Neuropsychological Assessment. Psychology has a long history of investigations into the relations between brain functioning and behavior. From a clinical perspective, the work of Goldstein and his associates provided the major impetus for diagnosing the effects on cognitive functioning of damage to specific areas of the brain. The findings by early researchers in what is now the field of learning disabilities led to theories of neurologic deficits as sources of learning problems; some children who had normal IQ but who were unable to read, calculate, spell, or write showed test patterns similar to those of individuals with confirmed brain injury. Since the term *learning disability* was made popular by Kirk in 1963, many definitions have implied or stated that learning disability is related to a neurological or organic dysfunction in cerebral processing (Coles, 1978). Children were labeled as minimally brain damaged or neurologically impaired on the basis of their performance on a number of sensory-motor, perceptual, and verbal tests, where the test profiles suggested soft signs (as contrasted in neurologically confirmed signs) of such dysfunction. Many tests used by learning disabilities diagnosticians are interpreted in this way, although these tests were not developed for that purpose (Coles, 1978).

The use of such tests as the WISC-R, Bender Visual-Motor Gestalt Test, Benton Visual Retention Test, or the Wepman Auditory Discrimination Test to infer brain damage encouraged what Maloney and Ward (1976, p. 211) called the unitary concept of organicity or organic brain damage: "brain damage is thought to cause a distinctive pattern of behavior [measured by tests] regardless of the cause, location, extent, or other circumstances regarding lesion and thus is a unitary or unidimensional concept." The unitary view contradicts the wealth of data attesting to the complexity of brain dysfunction and contributes to simplistic explanations of complex behavior (Coles, 1978).

However, neuropsychologists have made advances in the development of assessment instruments that demonstrate accuracy in the diagnosis of specific brain injury. According to Maloney and Ward (1976, p. 272), "Results . . . hold great promise for the development of procedures which will effectively assess the complex effects of damage to the brain." The best-validated and most representative battery presently in use is the Halsted-Reitan Neuropsychological Assessment Battery (Reitan, 1969; Reitan and Davison, 1974). This battery is composed of a number of separate tests, with the following usually included for assessments: Halsted Category Test, Speech-Sounds Perception Test, Seashore Rhythm Test, Tactual Performance Test, Trail Making Test, Aphasia Screening Test, Halsted Finger Tapping Test, and Lateral Dominance Test (Golden, 1979). A complete description of these tests and procedures for administering and scoring them are available in Reitan and Davison (1974). The tests measure a variety of specific skills and abilities, including deductive reasoning, auditory perception, concentration, attention, sequential and simultaneous functioning, motor speed, spatial visualization, kinesthesis, manual dexterity, and coordination.

Golden (1979) reviews studies that provide evidence of the construct and diagnostic validity of the tests included in this battery. Specific and accurate detection of lesion sites, size, and impact has been demonstrated. Differential diagnosis of tumors, head traumas, cerebrovascular disorders, epilepsy, and Parkinson's disease has also been validated against neurologic and surgical criteria. Maloney and Ward (1976, p. 276) cite studies demonstrating that the Halsted-Reitan battery has a higher correct classification rate than evaluations using angiograms, pneumoencephalograms, brain scans, and electroencephalograms. Thus, the clinical and empirical base of this battery seems firmly established.

There is also evidence that many of the tests developed by Halsted and Reitan have only low to moderate correlations with IQ and other general ability indicators (Golden, 1979). The tests therefore can contribute unique information about cognitive functioning that is not confounded with general ability as the ITPA and the Bender could not. Some recent evidence also suggests that several of the tests in the Halsted-Reitan battery are factorially separate from an ability-achievement factor loaded highly by group IQ and achievement test scores (Loveless and Hennessy, 1980).

To date, most validity studies of the Halsted-Reitan battery have used clinical populations rather than school children. The few studies that focus on diagnosis of learning problems give tentative support to its usefulness in more precise differential diagnosis (Loveless, 1981). If the hypothesized link between cerebral dysfunction and learning problems is to be validated, the more refined and sophisticated techniques developed by Reitan and other neuropsychologists will have to replace the imprecise measures presently used.

It is not likely, however, that such batteries as the Halsted-Reitan will become widely used, because of the time, complexity, and expense involved in administering and scoring the measures. A full evaluation, including the WISC-R, generally requires several one- to two-hour testing sessions spread over several days. To some extent, the time requirements may be so great as compared with the likely gain that school officials will discourage its use. In addition, some clumsy, large, complicated, and costly equipment must be bought and maintained. This factor may increase reluctance to use the scale. The scoring and interpretation of results requires specific training, and although Reitan offers workshops for instruction, considerable expertise needs to be developed. In spite of these administrative and procedural concerns, the growing validation literature on neuropsychological assessment may at some point force diagnosticians to include such batteries in any effort made to attribute diminished academic performance to organic factors. This evidence may "allow the clinician to depend on proven relationships within and between tests to reach conclusions about diagnosis rather than depend on clinical judgment" (Golden, 1979, p. 197). It was shown earlier that a similar claim cannot be made for most other widely used tests.

Multicomponent Latent Trait Analysis. Of the three assessment models that are likely to gain acceptance in the future, the multicomponent latent trait analysis model is the least well formulated, but it offers the greatest possible relevance to school-related diagnosis. The model may be an answer to Cronbach's call (1957, 1975) for an integration of the findings and methodologies of experimental and individual difference theories in psychology in order to understand complex human behaviors better. Because the model is still in the very early stages of development and many important aspects of it have yet to be published, it will be possible here to give only a broad description and to suggest where the model may prove useful in the future.

The term multicomponent latent trait analysis was used in two recent studies reported by Whitely (1980, 1981) to describe her attempt to bridge cognitive component process theories of intelligence with the most recent advance in psychometric theory, latent trait analysis. Component theories have been proposed by Carroll (1976), Glaser (1977), and Sternberg (1977, 1980). Cognitive components are viewed as "elementary information process[es] that operate upon internal representations of objects and symbols" (Sternberg, 1980, p. 6). They represent the processing operations, memory stores, and strategies used in problem solving. The highly specific components, which are experimentally validated, are thought to operate in most individuals who perform the task. There appears to be at least some similarity between the highly specific components hypothesized by component theorists and the more general cognitive operations described by Piagetian researchers. Both Piagetian and cognitive component theories describe general rules and procedures required to perform complex cognitive tasks, but, for the most part, the models are not concerned with individual differences in the ability to execute those rules and procedures.

Whitely's (1980, 1981) paradigm represents an attempt to account for individual differences by combining an understanding of the operations required for task performance with methodologies developed recently to assess item and subject characteristics that explain individual differences in test performance; in particular, with latent trait analysis and covariance modeling procedures. The cognitive components are viewed as separate, identifiable constructs that operate together in some predictable manner to determine successful task performance on test items. If systematic individual differences on components can be assessed, then specific and useful information is available for explaining individual performance differences on ability or achievement test items. Present assessment procedures can predict individual differences in performance with a reasonable degree of accuracy, but they do not specify what contributes to those differences. In contrast, Whitely has computed latent trait estimates of ability and decomposed ability test items into already validated cognitive components to describe the underlying dimension tapped by an ability or aptitude measure (Whitely, 1981).

A second aspect of Whitely's model may have an effect on individual assessment. She has developed a procedure for assessing cognitive component abilities that produces information specific to an individual. Such information has direct meaning for individual instruction. Not only can performance be assessed on a test item but information can also be obtained about individual differences on the underlying cognitive components by direct measurement of performance on these components. "Individual response to an intact item is a joint function of person ability and item difficulty on a set of underlying process components" (Whitely, 1981, p. 73). Three requirements necessary to assure the construct validity of these underlying cognitive process components are cited by Whitely. The first requirement is that "the component abilities should represent an empirically meaningful subdivision of the aptitude test score" (1981, p. 79). Essentially, this requires that more than one component should make a significant contribution to prediction of performance on an item. If only one component can explain the score variance on an item, there is no purpose in delineating components.

The second requirement is that the "component abilities should account for the external validity of the aptitude test . . . cognitive components should account for both the intercorrelations between separate aptitude tests and the correlation of aptitude with learning and achievement" (Whitely, 1981, p. 80). If this requirement can be demonstrated, Whitely suggests that a new structure of intellect based on construct valid component correlations, will have been found.

The third requirement is the most important for the diagnostic use of tests. "Component abilities should have differential validity in predicting learning under different conditions . . . . If component abilities do *not* have differential validity, little practical utility is gained by subdividing aptitudes into components" (Whitely, 1981, pp. 80–81).

Whitely (1980) reported the results of an investigation undertaken in part to test these three requirements. Two types of aptitude test items, verbal analogies and verbal classification, and six previously validated cognitive component measures were studied, using data obtained from 104 college students. The six cognitive components were assessed by readministering the aptitude test items on a second occasion where "each item was presented as a series of subtasks in which each subtask response reflected a different component process" (Whitely, 1980, p. 753). Scores on image construction, response evaluation, and event recovery were obtained from the classification and analogies tests. The item scores were used to estimate latent trait aptitude scores. These scores, the component scores, and ACT (American College Testing Program Examination) achievement scores in four content areas were analyzed to determine whether the requirements of the model were met. Whitely's results gave support to the multicomponent latent trait process in that the cognitive components were able to "model individual differences in verbal aptitude, . . . decompose test validity (that is, explain correlations with external measures), and . . . differentially predict achievement" on the ACT achievement measures (Whitely, 1980, p. 750). These very preliminary findings suggest that the multicomponent latent trait model may play a significant role in differential diagnosis of learning problems.

It must be emphasized that this is still an emerging field and that more research is needed to identify and validate more complex cognitive components. It seems, however, that Whitely has responded to some of the cautions raised by Carroll (1980) in speaking to the limitations of cognitive component analysis. Components can be identified that generalized over some, but not all, tasks, and differential predictions of achievement were validated. The benefit of Whitely's work for the assessment specialist is that she has demonstrated that critical cognitive components which jointly affect performance can be assessed separately. Such assessment can lead to the diagnosis of highly specific person deficiencies or weaknesses that interfere with mastery of academic skills. The model may make possible a truly diagnostic-prescriptive approach to the remediation of learning problems.

Conclusion

The likelihood that present practice in school abilities assessment will change soon is not great. Almost a half century of training and clinical experience lies behind traditional procedures. Thousands of school psychologists, diagnostic specialists, and special educators have accumulated a vast amount of rich data and insight to support their practices. Just as the analyses of clinical judgment by Meehl (1959), Goldberg (1970), and Wiggins (1973) have not dramatically changed personality assessment, the findings of such researchers as Arter and Jenkins (1979), Coles (1978), Reitan (1969), and Whitely (1981) may not soon change ability assessment practice.

An overwhelming amount of data attests to the validity of tests like the Stanford-Binet and the WISC-R for predicting scholastic performance. Binet's original intent when developing his scale is still being fulfilled: The tests predict performance well. Less compelling evidence exists to support their validity as diagnostic tools. Yet, it is not certain that they will be discarded, as Coles (1978) predicted.

It is likely, however, that newer, better-validated measures and models will make strong inroads and increase diagnostic capabilities. Current dissatisfaction may be reversed as these models become more widely known and used.

References

American Psychiatric Association. *Diagnostic and Statistical Manual of Mental Disorders.* (3rd ed.) Washington, D.C.: American Psychiatric Association, 1980.

Anastasi, A. *Psychological Testing.* (4th ed.) New York: Macmillan, 1976.

Arter, J., and Jenkins, J. "Differential Diagnosis-Prescriptive Teaching: A Critical Appraisal." *Review of Educational Research,* 1979, *49* (4), 517–555.

Brody, E., and Brody, H. *Intelligence: Nature, Determinants, and Consequences.* New York: Academic Press, 1976.

Budoff, M. "Measuring Learning Potential: An Alternative to the Traditional Intelligence Test." In C. R. Gredler (Ed.), *Ethical and Legal Factors in the Practice of School Psychology.* Philadelphia: Temple University Press, 1975.

Buros, O. *The Eighth Mental Measurements Yearbook.* Vol. 1. Highland Park, N.J.: Gryphon Press, 1978.

Carroll, J. "Psychometric Tests as Cognitive Tasks: A New 'Structure of Intellect.'" In L. Resnick (Ed.), *The Nature of Intelligence.* Hillsdale, N.J.: Erlbaum, 1976.

Carroll, J. "Remarks on Sternberg's 'Factor Theories of Intelligence Are All Right Almost.'" *Educational Researcher,* 1980, *9* (8), 14–18.

Coles, G. "The Learning Disabilities Test Battery: Empirical and Social Issues." *Harvard Educational Review,* 1978, *48* (3), 313–340.

Cronbach, L. "The Two Disciplines of Scientific Psychology." *American Psychologist,* 1957, *12,* 671–684.

Cronbach, L. "Test Validation." In R. Thorndike (Ed.), *Educational Measurement.* Washington, D.C.: American Educational Research Association, 1971.

Cronbach, L. "Beyond the Two Disciplines of Scientific Psychology." *American Psychologist,* 1975, *30,* 116–127.

Feuerstein, R. *The Dynamic Assessment of Retarded Learners.* Baltimore, Md.: University Park Press, 1979.

Glaser, R. *Adaptive Education: Individual Diversity and Learning.* New York: Holt, Rinehart and Winston, 1977.

Goldberg, L. "Man Versus Model of Man: A Rationale Plus Evidence for a Method of Improving Clinical Inferences." *Psychological Bulletin,* 1970, *73,* 422–432.

Golden, C. *Clinical Interpretation of Objective Psychological Tests.* New York: Grune and Stratton, 1979.

Jensen, A. R. "How Much Can We Boost IQ and Scholastic Achievement?" *Harvard Educational Review,* 1969, *39* (1), 1–123.

Jensen, A. *Bias in Mental Testing.* New York: Free Press, 1980.

Kaufman, A. "Factor Analysis of the WISC-R at Eleven Age Levels Between 6½ and 16½ Years." *Journal of Consulting and Clinical Psychology,* 1975, *43* (2), 135–147.

Kaufman, A. "A New Approach to the Interpretation of Test Scatter on the WISC-R." *Journal of Learning Disabilities,* 1976, *9* (3), 160–168.

Lidz, C. S. *Improving Assessment of School Children: A Guide to Evaluating Cognitive, Emotional, and Physical Problems.* San Francisco: Jossey-Bass, 1981.

Loveless, E. "The Specific Language Disabilities and Neuropsychological Model." Paper presented at the annual meeting of the Eastern Educational Research Association, Philadelphia, March 1981.

Loveless, E., and Hennessy, J. "The Use of Factor Analysis to Identify Subgroups of Dyslexic and Learning Disabled Children." Paper presented at the annual meeting of the Eastern Educational Research Association, Norfolk, Va., March 1980.

Lumsden, J. "Review of the Illinois Tests of Psycholinguistic Abilities." In O. Buros (Ed.), *The Eighth Mental Measurements Yearbook.* Vol. 1. Highland Park, N.J.: Gryphon Press, 1978.

Maloney, M., and Ward, M. *Psychological Assessment: A Conceptual Approach.* New York: Oxford University Press, 1976.

Matarazzo, J. *Wechsler's Measurement and Appraisal of Adult Intelligence.* (5th ed.) Baltimore, Md.: Williams & Wilkins. 1972.

Meehl, P. "A Comparison of Clinicians with Five Statistical Methods of Identifying Psychotic MMPI Profiles." *Journal of Counseling Psychology,* 1959, *6,* 102–109.

Mercer, J. *Labeling the Mentally Retarded.* Berkeley: University of California Press, 1973.

Mercer, J. *SOMPA Conceptual and Technical Manual.* New York: Psychological Corporation, 1978.

Messick, S. "Potential Uses of Noncognitive Measurement in Education." *Journal of Educational Psychology,* 1979, *71* (3), 281–292.

Popoff-Warner, L. "The Relationship Between IQ, SES, Adaptive Behavior, and Performance on a Measure of Learning Potential." Unpublished doctoral dissertation, Fordham University, 1980.

Reitan, R. *Manual for the Administration of Neuropsychological Test Batteries for Adults and Children.* Indianapolis: R. Reitan, 1969.

Reitan, R., and Davison, L. (Eds.). *Clinical Neuropsychology.* Washington, D.C.: Winston, 1974.

Sattler, J. *Assessment of Children's Intelligence.* (Revised reprint.) Philadelphia: Saunders, 1974.

Spearman, C. *The Abilities of Man: Their Nature and Measurement.* New York: Macmillan, 1927.

Sternberg, R. "Component Processes in Analogical Reasoning." *Psychological Review,* 1977, *31,* 356–378.

Sternberg, R. "Factor Theories of Intelligence Are All Right Almost." *Educational Researcher,* 1980, *9* (8), 6–13, 18.

Wechsler, D. *Manual for the Wechsler Intelligence Scale for Children, Revised.* New York: Psychological Corporation, 1974.

Weiderholt, J. "Review of the Illinois Tests of Psycholinguistic Abilities." In O. Buros (Ed.), *The Eighth Mental Measurements Yearbook.* Vol. 1. Highland Park, N.J.: Gryphon Press, 1978.

Whitely, S. "Modeling Aptitude Test Validity from Cognitive Components." *Journal of Educational Psychology,* 1980, *72* (6), 750–769.

Whitely, S. "Measuring Aptitude Processes with Multicomponent Latent Trait Models." *Journal of Educational Measurement,* 1981, *18* (2), 67–84.

Wiggins, J. *Personality and Prediction: Principles of Personality Assessment.* Reading, Mass.: Addison-Wesley, 1973.

James J. Hennessy is associate professor and coordinator of the counseling and personnel services program in the Graduate School of Education, Fordham University, and a consulting psychologist in a public school program for emotionally disturbed children in Suffolk County, New York.

Prediction of grades from measures of students' aptitudes and their treatment
by teachers (for example, encouragement and monitoring) are reported for
the same students' eighth- and tenth-grade performances. Patterns of
aptitudes vary somewhat between subject matter domains and vary markedly
between subgroups defined by teacher treatments. Close monitoring
and warm encouragement, in a structured setting, appear to provide the
most conducive learning situation for students.

Aptitudes as Predictors of Achievement Moderated by Teacher Effect

Barbara Hummel-Rossi

Why do some students do better in school than others? This question has occupied the efforts of many in education, psychology, and sociology. Early researchers examined the relation between student achievement and a few isolated measures of aptitude, prior achievement, and personality. Building on their work, today's researchers have come to appreciate the complexity of student achievement and the necessity of understanding individual differences within the context of the student's traits and the social systems of his school and family. Against this background, a comprehensive study of student achievement in junior high school students was undertaken, and its results are reported in this chapter.

Background

A primary concern in the study of student achievement is how aptitudes influence performance. Correlations between aptitude and achievement measures generally range from .20 to .70, clustering between .40 and .50. However, results are quite dependent on the population from which the sample has been drawn and the particular aptitude measures used. For example,

P. Merrifield (Ed.). *New Directions for Testing and Measurement: Measuring Human Abilities*, no. 12.
San Francisco: Jossey-Bass, December 1981.

scores from the Wechsler Intelligence Scale for Children, Revised (Wechsler, 1974) and scores from the Differential Aptitude Test (Bennett, Seashore, and Wesman, 1974) relate to student achievement differently, because the nature of what is measured, the scoring procedures, and the administration methods all differ.

A relatively recent approach to the study of aptitudes and achievement has been to identify highly specific aptitudes theorized to be necessary for success in a particular subject area and to relate these aptitudes to achievement in that area. This approach is based on the theory that different curricula and even different instructional approaches demand different abilities and that these abilities should be identified if learning is to be maximized. The work of Cronbach and Snow (1977) and Snow (1976), who have studied individual differences and aptitude treatment interaction, reflects this approach. It is also the approach used in the work reported here.

The theoretical orientation toward aptitudes of this investigation was based on Merrifield's TETRA model, as described in another chapter; to summarize, in that model, Merrifield defines two tetrahedrons, one for thought processes and one for thought content. Four basic thought processes — transforming, remembering, evaluating, and generating — define the four points of the thought processes tetrahedron. These thought processes operate on the thought content tetrahedron, the four points of which are defined as self, other persons, ideas, and forms. Edges and faces of both tetrahedrons are also defined.

Each individual is theorized to have a unique pattern of aptitude strengths and weaknesses that make learning easier in certain subject areas than in others. The importance of identifying the relation between these specific aptitudes and subject-area achievement is obvious: Students with a weak aptitude pattern can be given special attention and remedial help, and students with a strong aptitude pattern can be given more advanced or supplementary work.

In operationalizing and assessing aptitudes, we borrowed heavily from the fine work of Ekstrom (1973) and of Ekstrom, French, and Harman (1976); these researchers identified tests that could serve as markers for established cognitive factors. Because the TETRA model evolved from Merrifield's work with the Guilford Structure-of-Intellect Model and because many of the aptitude tests identified by Ekstrom, French, and Harman were based on Guilford's model or on other models, such as Cattell's (1963, 1971a), with which cross-comparisons of cognitive factors were possible, the measurement instruments used to assess aptitudes were consistent with the TETRA model of aptitudes.

Aptitudes do not operate in isolation, and certain of an individual's personality characteristics can be important to his academic achievement. Such personality traits include needs for achievement, order, and endurance (Gebhart and Hoyt, 1958; Krug, 1959; Merrill and Murphy, 1959); freedom from nervous symptoms (Nason, 1958); and good work habits and adjustment and acceptance of adult standards (d'Heurle, Mellinger, and Haggard, 1959). As with aptitudes, the nature of the relation between personality traits and achievement is highly dependent upon how the trait is defined and operationalized; inconsistencies in research findings are often due to differences in assessment instruments as well as to differences in the population and research design. For example, consider one of the personality traits used in this study, Emotionally Stable Versus Affected by Feelings (Cattell, 1968). According to the analyses of French (1973) and Dermen, French, and Harman (1978), the Cattell measure includes three item categories: emotionally stable versus emotionally sensitive; optimistic versus worrying; and healthy feeling versus hypochondriac. Several other scales include all three categories. Yet, a number of scales with names that sound much like *emotionally stable* include only one or two of the three categories, and one scale with the name Emotional Stability seems to be a measure of neuroticism. Given these differences in the operationalization of just one construct, the reader can understand why no definitive statements about the relation between personality traits and achievement have been made.

Research has shown that particular personality traits and aptitudes can be related to performance in a subject area. For example, d'Heurle, Mellinger, and Haggard (1959) found that gifted third graders who were high in mathematics achievement were superior also in their ability to relate to adults and in their aptitude for symbol manipulation. In his research with a new medical school curriculum that required considerable cooperative effort among students, Snow (1976) reported that high-ability students who liked to work independently did as well as or poorer than middle-ability students who liked interpersonal relations. In a study of achievement in statistics among college students, Elmore and Vasu (1980) found that masculinity-femininity of interest patterns and five measures of spatial-visualization were significantly related to achievement.

In deciding to include personality traits in the investigation reported here, we had to decide which theoretical approach to adopt. The path seemed to lead naturally to Cattell (1965, 1971a, 1971b). The High School Personality Questionnaire developed by Cattell (1968) was particularly suited to the population under study; also, it has broad coverage of personality traits and excellent psychometric qualities.

The student brings his aptitudes, personality traits, and prior learning to the school. How he applies these characteristics to learning is not just a product of how they function together but of how they function in the school setting. Each school has its own social system, and there are many components to the system. In this investigation, it was not possible to study all the components, so we decided to focus on just one important component, the teacher. Teachers treat students differently. They have expectations and preferences for different types of students, and these expectations and preferences can be related to their interaction with students. The literature on teacher expectations shows that student sex, name, ethnic background, physical attractiveness, socioeconomic status, and intelligence test results are some determinants of teacher expectations that subsequently can influence teacher behavior (Braun, 1976). Specifically, in research that asked teachers to rate narrative descriptions of students, it has been found that teachers prefer orderly, rigid, passive, and conforming students and that they reject assertive and active students (Feshbach, 1969; Good and Grouws, 1972; Helton, 1972). Teachers rate brighter students in a more favorable light (Barnard, Zimbardo, and Sarason, 1968), and their judgment of a student's ability is often correlated with their evaluation of the student's self-confidence, maturity, and ability to work without supervision (Willis, 1972). In studies of teacher-student interaction, teachers tend to praise more, criticize less, and respond more frequently to high-achieving students than they do to low-achieving students (Brophy and Good, 1970; Jeter and Davis, 1973). Responding to these findings, we decided to gain further knowledge of the relation between student achievement and teacher behavior by asking teachers how they treated each of their students. A three-category scale for teachers to use was developed.

In summary, if we want to know why Johnny fails and Jimmy passes, we need to know a great deal about Johnny and Jimmy. We need to know about their aptitudes, their personality traits, and what happens to them in the classroom. Little comprehensive research of this type has been undertaken, and our study responded to the need for such research. More than 200 junior high school students participating in an individualized instruction program were studied. The study had four goals: to develop a comprehensive aptitude battery of separable aptitudes theoretically related to the different curricula; to relate these aptitude measures and measures of student personality and sex to student achievement in different curricula; to reexamine these aptitudes, personality traits, and sex as predictors of achievement after a two-year span; and to examine the relation of teacher reports of treatment of students to student personality characteristics and student achievement.

The Samples

The setting for this investigation was an upper-middle-class suburb in a large metropolitan area. The junior high school in which the study was conducted had good facilities and attracted well-qualified teachers. This researcher spent considerable time in the school over a two-year period and was impressed by the dedication of most of the teachers, the involvement of the parents, and the excellent administration. The primary sample of the investigation was drawn from all the eighth graders. Seventy-one students were excluded from the sample either because they were not enrolled in the individualized instruction program (usually at the parents' request) or because their high absenteeism made testing impossible. Of the sample of 219 students between the ages of thirteen and fourteen, 110 were girls and 109 were boys.

The students were followed up two years later as tenth graders. Of the original sample, it was possible to obtain complete tenth-grade achievement data on 167 students, 90 girls and 77 boys. Data on the remaining students were not available because of normal attrition and differences in student course scheduling.

Twelve eighth-grade teachers, each with at least three years of teaching experience, participated in the study. Six were women, and six were men. In addition, for replication purposes, 221 seventh graders in the school were administered the aptitude and personality tests. Their teachers responded to the teacher treatment measures and achievement scores, and teacher-assigned grades were obtained.

The Assessment Instruments

Aptitude Assessment. The seventh- and eighth-grade curricula in language, mathematics, science, and social studies were analyzed with the TETRA model to determine which aptitudes were required for each area. For each curriculum area, every fifth daily lesson was examined. If there seemed to be a great deal of variability within a five-lesson sequence, a complete week of lessons was analyzed. A standard form, prepared by the author, was used for the analysis. The form included such information as prior achievements, facilitating aptitudes, and essential aptitudes. All learning materials, pretests, and posttests for the lesson were examined. Fortunately, few discrepancies were found between the aptitudes required for successful learning and the aptitudes ostensibly measured by the tests available. This is not always the case, and other researchers are cautioned not to overlook it.

Prior achievements were not of major concern, because individual instruction precludes advancement to the next stage unless successful performance has been demonstrated. Of course, there are differences between students who regularly meet the minimum criteria for advancement and students who regularly have perfect scores. However, much of this variability should be reflected in differences in aptitude scores. Continuity was found between the curricula of the seventh and eighth grades. Analyses were done by this author with assistance from a trained doctoral-level graduate student in educational psychology.

The most important aptitudes were identified, and, based upon validity and reliability considerations, eighteen tests were selected. Some tests were used as is, others were modified for the testing situation, and two were developed for the battery (see Figure 1 for description of tests). The intercorrelations among the tests were factored by alpha analysis, and the factors were rotated to a six-factor varimax solution. Based on the loadings and the construct validity of the tests, one test was selected from each of the four factors that had more than one measure loading at least .39. The first factor involved production of ideational systems; Word Grouping was chosen to represent this factor. The second factor represented general reasoning and evaluation of systems;

Figure 1. Description of Aptitude Tests

Card Rotations: Given a row of reflected and/or rotated drawings of the same form, decide which is the same, within rotation but not reflection, of the first form in the two (multiple-choice format).

Circle Reasoning: Given a set of four series of circles and dashes in which one circle is marked, educe the rule for the set and apply it to a fifth series (completion format).

Figure Analogies: Analogies test requiring eduction of a rule for changing one figure to another (such as proportionately smaller or color internal form) and application of the rule to a new figure (multiple-choice format).

Food Naming: Name foods beginning with each letter of the alphabet, in alphabetical order (completion format).

Gestalt Completion: Name objects represented by incomplete silhouettes (such as Gottschaldt figures) (completion format).

Identical Pictures: Given a row of outline forms, mark those identical to the first element in the row (multiple-choice format).

Learned Information: Immediately after reading several paragraphs preceded by instructions to remember the content, paraphrase the content in written production within a short time period (essay format).

Marking X's: On a page full of regularly arranged small squares, write an X in each square as rapidly as possible (completion format).

Number Group Naming: Given a series of numbers, write the name of the group to which all the numbers belong (for example, multiples of 7) (completion format).

Omelet Test: Given four letters, designate which is the initial letter of a word that includes all the letters (multiple-choice format).

Reading Backwards: Indicate ability to read backwards by doing simple tasks as directed (for example: rats a ward; answer:*) (completion format).

Ship Destination: Given rules involving distances between points on a grid and varying conditions, compute distance of specified trips (completion format).

Sign Changes: Given an equation, evaluate correctness of equation, and change arithmetic sign(s), if necessary, to make equation true (multiple-choice format).

Symbol Manipulation: Given defined symbols for logical relations (such as older than, and equality-inequality) evaluate the truth or falsity of symbolic statements (true-false format).

Word Arrangement: Using four given words, make as many different sentences as possible including all four (completion format).

Word Grouping: Given a group of fifteen names of objects, educe categories and demonstrate by correctly classifying them (completion format).

Word Recognition: After brief study of fifteen words, immediately indicate recall of them by checking them in a list of thirty words (check format).

Word Relations: Analogies test requiring eduction of a rule for forming one word from another (for example "not" from "ton") and applying the rule to a new word (multiple-choice format).

Figure Analogies was chosen. The third factor appeared to be verbal closure; the Omelet Test was chosen to represent it. The fourth factor was perceptual speed; the test chosen was Identical Pictures. Although Circle Reasoning had not led to the identification of any factors, it was also chosen because of the author's special interest in abstract reasoning. Reliabilities for the eighth-grade sample estimated from the Kuder-Richardson 21 (hereafter KR-21) formula were Word Grouping, .90; Figure Analogies, .80; Omelet Test, .77; Identical Pictures, .84; and Circle Reasoning, .62.

Personality Assessment. The Junior-Senior High School Personality Questionnaire (HSPQ) (Cattell, 1968) was used to assess personality. The HSPQ is designed for children between the ages of twelve and eighteen. It has fourteen scales, ten items per scale, and multiple-choice items with three alternatives (see Figure 2 for a description of these scales). Construct validity is

Figure 2. Description of Personality Traits

Alphabetic Designation of Factor	High Score Description[a]
A	Warm-hearted, outgoing, easygoing
B	Bright, high intelligence[b]
C	Emotionally stable, mature
D	Excitable, impatient, demanding
E	Assertive, aggressive, competitive
F	Enthusiastic, happy-go-lucky
G	Conscientious, persistent, staid
H	Adventurous, socially bold
I	Tender-minded, sensitive
J	Circumspect individualism, reflective
O	Apprehensive, self-reproaching
Q_2	Self-sufficient, resourceful
Q_3	Controlled, exacting will power
Q_4	Tense, driven, overwrought

[a]Descriptions from Cattell and Cattell (1969).
[b]A brief measure of "crystallized" general ability; a power, rather than a speed, measure of ability (Cattell, 1963).

supported by many factor analytic studies in different adolescent populations (Cattell and Cattell, 1969). Based on a sample of 120 ninth graders, the reliability of alternate forms over a six-month period ranged from .68 to .82.

The intercorrelations among the fourteen scales were factored, using principal factors with squared multiple correlations as communality estimates, iterated to four factors. Four second-stratum factors are suggested by Cattell and Cattell (1969). Examination of these four factors revealed that Bright dominated one of the factors but had an extremely low communality. A normalized varimax rotation was performed, which resulted in a correlation of − .84 between two factors. Given these findings, it was decided to do a graphic rotation to maximize three orthogonal hyperplanes. The resulting three factors can be described as: Factor I, Group-Involved (Exvia); Factor II, Anxious Insecurity; and Factor III, Heedless Individual Gratification (Assertiveness). Spearman-Brown estimates of reliability from the factor loadings were .66, .76, and .58, for Factors I, II, and III, respectively; Bright had a reliability of .71 as estimated by KR-21. For some analyses, the three factors and the individual scale Bright were used. For other analyses, a leading scale was chosen from each factor and used along with Bright. These three scales were Warm-Hearted versus Reserved for Factor I; Emotionally Stable versus Easily Upset for Factor II; and Tender-Minded versus Tough-Minded for Factor III. On the 219 eighth graders, KR-21 reliability estimates for these three scales were .60 for Warm-Hearted, .63 for Emotionally Stable, and .76 for Tender-Minded.

Achievement Assessment. The Stanford Achievement Test, Advanced (SAT) (Gardner and others, 1965) was one of the criteria for achievement. Its content validity has been widely accepted, and the reliabilities of its subtests and total score are consistently high. Three factors have been reported for this test (Gardner and others, 1965). In anticipation of this finding, the intercorrelations for the nine subtests obtained from the testing of the eighth-grade sample were factored using principal factor analysis. There was clearly only one factor: The eigenvalue for the first factor was 6.40 and for the second, .41 (Merrifield and Hummel-Rossi, 1976). Loadings for the nine subtests on the first factor were all in the .80s except for a .72 for the Spelling subtest.

Although the SAT criteria measures were highly correlated in this sample, they were used separately, as it is standard practice in education to use the individual SAT subtest scores for placement and counseling. In studying eighth-grade achievement, the Language, Mathematics Concepts, Science, and Social Science subtests were used as criteria. Reliability estimates on the eighth graders from KR-21 were .80 for Language, .83 for Mathematics Concepts, .74 for Science, and .78 for Social Science.

In the follow-up study of the students as tenth graders, our interest was in explaining tenth-grade achievement by first removing variance associated with prior knowledge. The Reading Comprehension (KR-21 reliability of .83) and the Mathematics Computation (KR-21 reliability of .79) subtests were chosen, as they represented the most fundamental achievement areas. Also used for some tenth-grade analyses were the Mathematics Application and Spelling subtests, with KR-21 reliabilities of .82 and .84, respectively.

The second criterion for achievement was teacher grades. As noted earlier, it is recognized that the reliability and validity of teacher grades are often questionable. However, despite their fallibility, teacher grades are widely used in high schools as determinants of success. Further, from the point of view of expectations, if teacher behaviors toward and evaluations of an individual student are consistent across teachers, the student may use this consistency as a basis for developing personal expectations about his own behavior and then act to fulfill them.

Teacher grades in language, mathematics, science, and social studies were obtained for all 219 eighth graders and for a subsample of this group ($n = 167$) as tenth graders. Cumulative end-of-year grades were converted from a letter grade to a numerical grade using a nine-point scale.

Teacher Treatment of Students. The Teacher Report of Treatment of Students (TRTS) was used to assess the manner in which teachers perceived how they interacted with students. It was developed by Hummel-Rossi and Merrifield to deepen the knowledge of teacher-student relationships provided by previous work on teacher feedback and expectations. The developers saw it as an exploratory instrument, and, quite honestly, they did not anticipate the surprising findings described in this chapter. The TRTS assesses three types of verbal and nonverbal teacher behavior toward students. These behaviors are theorized to be important in an individualized instruction setting. For each behavior, the teacher notes the degree on a five-point scale. The first assessment, Directing versus Eliciting, establishes the extent to which the teacher directs the student's entering behavior on new projects. The second assessment, Permissive versus Monitoring, reflects the teacher's degree of close supervision while the student works on the project. The third assessment, Encouraging versus Challenging, indicates the nature of the feedback that the teacher provides, which ranges from highly supportive to intellectually challenging.

Teachers responded for students for whom they had major responsibility. Each student was rated by three teachers, and the three ratings were added. Twelve teachers rated the students.

Preliminary analyses showed that the Directing versus Eliciting and Permissive versus Monitoring assessments were probably measures of the same dimension of teacher behavior but with opposite polarity. Therefore, the Permissive versus Monitoring measure was subtracted from the Directing versus Eliciting measure to create a new measure, Directing-Monitoring versus Eliciting-Permissive, hereafter referred to as the Eliciting-Permissive measure. Thus, two teacher reports of treatment of students were used in the analysis, Eliciting-Permissive and Encouraging versus Challenging, which will hereafter be referred to as the Challenging scale. Further, preliminary analyses of the correlations between individual teacher TRTS measures and the HSPQ measures revealed that the patterns of two teachers were not homogeneous. Thus, the measures provided by these two teachers were eliminated, as the intent was to pool ratings. Consequently, for 109 students, two rather than three teacher TRTS ratings were available, and a weighted sum was derived for these students. The usual reliability computations could not be made. However, from the analysis reported here that related these two TRTS measures to the personality traits, estimates are available from the communalities as lower bounds, and these gave reliability estimates of .64 for Eliciting-Permissive and .67 for Challenging.

The Students as Eighth Graders

Considering first the SAT subtest scores as criteria for achievement, four separate stepwise regression analyses were run, using the SAT Language, Mathematics Concepts, Science, and Social Science subtests as criteria. The independent variables were the five aptitude measures (Word Grouping, Figure Analogies, Circle Reasoning, Omelet Test, and Identical Pictures), sex, and the four personality measures (Emotionally Stable, Tender-Minded, Warm-Hearted, and Bright). The aptitude measures were forced into the equation in a combined stepwise, hierarchical fashion. First the aptitude set was given highest priority, then the set of sex and the personality traits. Within each set, the data determined the sequence of the variables. Results are presented in Table 1. Language was best predicted ($R^2 = .53$),* Mathematics was close behind ($R^2 = .52$), and Science and Social Science were last ($R^2 = .48$ for each). The results for the four criteria were consistent, and one discussion suffices. Two aptitude measures, Figure Analogies and Word Grouping, provided multiple determination coefficients of $R^2 = .39$ ($R = .62$) or higher. The inclusion of Circle Reasoning and the Omelet Test added about 2 percent. Identical Pictures added no significant variance. Following the aptitude tests, the addition of sex and personality traits added little to the prediction. However, note the large correlations of Bright with the criteria. All are .46 or higher. When Bright was considered as an aptitude, not as a personality trait, it became the third most important predictor. The remaining personality traits and sex all had low zero-order correlations (r) with the criteria.

The two most noteworthy findings of this study are the importance of Figure Analogies and Word Grouping and the unimportance of sex to the prediction of achievement. Figure Analogies and Word Grouping require only about twenty minutes of testing time, yet they provided in this study predic-

*R^2 denotes the proportion of variance in the criterion which is predicted by the indicated combination of aptitude scores and other measures; R denotes the coefficient of multiple correlation; and r denotes the zero-order coefficient of correlation between two variables only (for example, the criterion and one of the predictors with r denoting its absolute value, magnitude not considering sign).

Table 1. Prediction of Eighth-Grade SAT Achievement from Aptitudes, Sex, and Personality Traits

Measure	Zero-Order L[c]	M	S	SS	Increments to R^2 [b] L	M	S	SS
Figure Analogies	.51	.58	.55	.54	.11	.34	.30	.29
Word Grouping	.58	.50	.47	.50	.33	.10	.09	.11
Circle Reasoning	.41	.38	.33	.38	.03	.01	.01	.02
Omelet Test	.49	.42	.38	.38	.03	.01	.00	.00
Identical Pictures	.35	.32	.32	.25	.00	.00	.00	.00
Bright	.47	.49	.46	.48	.02	.03	.03	.03
Sex (Boy=0; Girl=1)	.17	-.08	-.12	-.07	.01	.02	.03	.02
Emotionally Stable	.11	.09	.14	.17	.00	.01	.00	.01
Tender-minded	.09	-.02	-.06	-.05	.00	.00	.00	.00
Warm-hearted	.20	.16	.17	.13	.00	.00	.01	.00
Multiple R^2=					.53	.52	.48	.48
"Shrunken" R^2 =					.51	.50	.46	.46

Correlations[a]

Note: N = 219; all values rounded to nearest hundreth.

[a]For zero-order correlations in this table, each considered separately, p < .01 for $|r| > .18$; for increments to R^2, p < .05 for increments > .01, for all predictors.
[b]Aptitudes forced in first, then sex and personality.
[c]L denotes Language; M, Mathematics Concepts; S, Science; and SS, Social Science.

tive power equal to that of many of the longer, frequently administered intelligence tests used in junior high schools.

That sex was not a significant predictor was surprising. Males are frequently found to be superior in mathematics, and females, to be superior in languages. However, this was not the case here. Further, sex did not function as a moderator. No differences in within-sex correlations of predictors and criteria were found. Also, the low zero-order correlations between sex and Emotionally Stable (r = .17) and sex and Warm-Hearted (r = .23) are not consistent with earlier work (Cattell and Cattell, 1969) but confirm more recent work (Hakstian and Cattell, 1975). Consistent with much research, girls (coded 1) were found to be more sensitive and dependent, whereas boys (coded 0) were more unsentimental and independent (based on r of .57 between sex and Tender-Minded).

Considering next eighth-grade teacher-assigned grades as the criterion for achievement, separate regression analyses were done for each subject area. The corresponding subject-area SAT was forced into each analysis first to remove variation that could be attributed to achievement. Then, five aptitude measures (Word Grouping, Figure Analogies, Circle Reasoning, Omelet Test, and Identical Pictures), personality traits (Warm-Hearted, Emotionally Stable, Tender-Minded, and Bright), sex, and TRTS measures (Eliciting-Permissive and Challenging) were allowed to enter, according to their relation with the criterion. The SAT measures removed between 14 and 31 percent of the variance in grades (see Table 2). A startling finding was that, after variation in grades had been removed by achievement, the next best predictor for each subject area was the TRTS measure, Eliciting-Permissive. Eliciting-Permissive accounted for between 24 and 31 percent of the variance in grades.

Table 2. Prediction of Eighth-Grade Teacher-Assigned Grades from TRTS, Aptitudes, and Personality Traits

Measure	Mean	S.D.	Rel[a]	Correlations with Grades[b]							
				Zero-order				Increments to R^2			
				L[c]	M	S	SS	L	M	S	SS
SAT Language	103.72	27.02	.80	.51	.51	.60	.47	.26*	-	-	-
SAT Math Concepts	99.02	18.95	.83	.42	.53	.50	.35	-	.28*	-	-
SAT Science	103.24	22.22	.74	.29	.35	.55	.31	-	-	.31*	-
SAT Social Science	101.03	19.36	.78	.39	.48	.57	.37	-	-	-	.14*
E-P	.04	6.61	.64	.76	.75	.71	.62	.31*	.31*	.24*	.24*
Challenging	8.82	2.22	.67	.30	.38	.27	.26	.01	.02*	.00	.01
Identical Pictures	62.75	13.43	.84	.16	.23	.35	.12	.01*	.00	.01*	.01
Circle Reasoning	6.74	3.05	.62	.31	.33	.32	.18	.00	.00	.00	.00
Omelet	17.91	5.46	.77	.22	.29	.28	.14	.00	.00	.00	.00
Word Grouping	38.47	13.02	.90	.35	.34	.44	.28	.00	.00	.00	.00
Figure Analogies	16.54	5.74	.80	.28	.39	.36	.21	.00	.00	.00	.00
Sex (Boy=0, Girl=1)	.50	.50	1.00	.24	.11	.10	.22	.00	.00	.00	.01
Warm	10.89	3.50	.60	.19	.11	.07	.14	.00	.00	.01	.00
Tender	9.27	4.40	.76	.19	.04	.06	.07	.00	.01	.00	.01
Stable	9.88	3.68	.63	.10	.14	.15	.23	.00	.00	.00	.02*
Bright	6.81	1.91	.71	.37	.40	.42	.31	.00	.00	.00	.00
							Multiple R^2=.60	.62	.58	.44	
							"Shrunken" Multiple R^2=.57	.60	.56	.40	

Note: N = 219; all values rounded to nearest hundreth.

[a]Reliability estimated from KR-21 formula for all variables except E-P, Challenging, and Sex. For E-P and Challenging reliability estimated from communalities.
[b]For zero-order correlations in this table, $p < .01$ for $|r| > .18$. For increments to R^2, $p < .05$ for increments $> .01$; significant predictors noted with *.
[c]L denotes Language Grades; M, Mathematics Grades; S, Science Grades; and SS, Social Studies Grades.

The TRTS Challenging variable was less important. Taken together, the SAT and the Eliciting-Permissive measures accounted for at least 55 percent of the variation in language, mathematics, and science grades and for 38 percent of the variance in social studies grades. Contribution by the remaining variables, particularly the aptitudes, was minimal. These results indicated that teachers rewarded students who required little direction or monitoring of their work with high grades, while lower grades were assigned to students who needed more direction.

It had been anticipated that the TRTS measures would be important predictors, but it was not expected that the Eliciting-Permissive measure would be more strongly related to grades than the aptitude measures. Note that the correlations between teacher-assigned grades and the Eliciting-Permissive measures are .76 for language grades, .75 for mathematics grades, .71 for science grades, and .62 for social studies grades. The relations between Eliciting-Permissive and the SAT measures were also strong: .62 for language, .53 for Mathematics Concepts, .52 for Science, and .54 for Social Studies. Corresponding correlations for the Challenging scale were in the .30s. Exploring these relations further, two more sets of analyses were run in which just the five aptitude measures, sex, the two TRTS measures, and the three personality traits were considered. Bright was removed because of its substantial intercorrelations with the aptitudes. In the first set of analyses, the variables were allowed to enter the regression equation in a stepwise fashion, according to their relation to the criterion. In the second set of analyses, the Eliciting-Permissive variable was forced into the regression equation as the last variable, and the other variables entered the equation in a stepwise manner, according to their relation with the criterion.

In the first analyses set, the Eliciting-Permissive variable was the strongest predictor of grades, accounting for 37 to 56 percent of the variation. The remaining variables accounted for little (see Table 3). Even when the Eliciting-Permissive variable was forced into the analysis as the last variable in the second analyses set, it still accounted for the largest amount of variance in teacher-assigned grades: 35 percent in language grades, 34 percent in mathematics grades, 26 percent in science grades, and 23 percent in social studies grades. Word Grouping and Figure Analogies, which had been such strong predictors of SAT achievement, accounted for substantially less variance in teacher-assigned grades. In the second analysis set, in which Eliciting-Permissive was forced in as the last predictor, Word Grouping was the best predictor of teacher-assigned grades in language ($R^2 = .12$), science ($R^2 = .19$), and social studies ($R^2 = .08$) and the second best predictor in mathematics (R^2 increment = .05). Figure Analogies was the best predictor in mathematics ($R^2 = .15$). Circle Reasoning emerged as the second best predictor in language and science (R^2 increment = .06 for both), and the personality characteristic Emotionally Stable was the second best predictor in social studies (R^2 increment = .02).

Table 3. Prediction of Eighth-Grade Teacher-Assigned Grades from TRTS, Aptitudes, and Personality Traits

Measure	First Analysis[a] Increments to R^2 [c]				Second Analysis[b] Increments to R^2 [c]			
	L[d]	M	S	SS	L	M	S	SS
Eliciting-Permissive	.57*	.56*	.50*	.37*	.35*	.34*	.26*	.23*
	(1)	(1)	(1)	(1)	(11)	(11)	(11)	(11)
Challenging	.00	.02*	.00	.00	.00	.00	.00	.00
	(5)	(2)	(10)	(8)	(10)	(8)	(6)	(8)
Word Grouping	.00	.00	.02*	.00	.12*	.05*	.19*	.08*
	(3)	(11)	(2)	(7)	(1)	(2)	(1)	(1)
Figure Analogies	.00	.01	.00	.00	.02	.15*	.02*	.02
	(10)	(4)	(9)	(11)	(4)	(1)	(3)	(4)
Circle Reasoning	.00	.00	.00	.00	.06*	.03*	.06*	.01
	(4)	(5)	(6)	(10)	(2)	(3)	(2)	(5)
Omelet Test	.00	.00	.00	.00	.00	.00	.00	.00
	(9)	(6)	(11)	(6)	(9)	(6)	(9)	(9)
Identical Pictures	.01	.00	.01	.01	.00	.00	.02	.00
	(2)	(9)	(4)	(5)	(7)	(9)	(4)	(7)
Sex	.00	.00	.02*	.01	.03*	.01	.00	.04*
	(6)	(10)	(3)	(3)	(3)	(5)	(10)	(3)
Stable	.00	.00	.00	.02*	.01	.01	.01	.04*
	(11)	(8)	(7)	(2)	(5)	(4)	(5)	(2)
Tender-Minded	.00	.01*	.00	.01	.00	.00	.00	.00
	(8)	(3)	(8)	(4)	(6)	(7)	(8)	(6)
Warm-Hearted	.00	.00	.00	.00	.00	.00	.00	.00
	(7)	(7)	(5)	(9)	(8)	(10)	(7)	(10)
Multiple R^2 =					.60	.61	.56	.44
"Shrunken" Multiple R^2 =					.58	.59	.54	.41

Note: N = 219; all values rounded to nearest hundreth.

[a]Order determined by highest partial correlation, sequence entered in parentheses.

[b]E-P forced in as last variable; resulting sequence entered in parenthesis.

[c]For increments to R^2, $p < .05$ for increments $> .01$; significant predictors noted *.

[d]L denotes Language Grades; M, Mathematics Grades; S, Science Grades; and SS, Social Studies Grades.

A replication study was performed using the 221 seventh-grade students. The results were about the same as those for the eighth graders. Eliciting-Permissive again emerged as the most powerful predictor, accounting for 31 to 76 percent of the variation in teacher-assigned grades in language, mathematics, science, and social studies when the predictors were the five aptitudes, sex, three personality traits, and two TRTS measures.

It was discouraging to find that a student's grades were more strongly related to how the teacher reported treating him than to the student's aptitudes or prior achievement. One must question the motivation of rewarding with high grades students who, the teacher believes, need the least amount of direction and supervision. Yet, these results are consistent with prior research, which has shown that teacher ratings of student ability are positively correlated with teacher evaluations of student attention, self-confidence, and ability to work without supervision (Willis, 1972).

The importance of the Eliciting-Permissive measure in prediction of grades indicated the need for further investigation. To gain insight into the relation between teachers' reports of how they treat students (TRTS measures) and student personality traits, the two TRTS measures were extended into the space defined by the three personality factors and Bright (Hummel-Rossi and Merrifield, 1977). In this type of regression analysis, the beta weights correspond to the factor loadings of the TRTS variables. The Eliciting-Permissive scale was most strongly related to Anxious Insecurity (loading of .55) and Heedless Individual Gratification (loading of − .54). The Challenging scale was strongly related to Anxious Insecurity (loading of − .66) and related to Bright (loading of .42). These results are presented in Table 4.

From these teachers' reports of how they treated their students, it appears that the teachers were highly directive and monitoring with apprehensive, insecure, and anxious students. They used more permissive techniques with self-assured, emotionally stable students. Also, they were highly directive and monitoring with the tough-minded, enthusiastic students and used eliciting-permissive methods with tender-minded, sober students. In giving feedback, teachers provided a clear intellectual challenge to emotionally stable, undemonstrative students and to bright students and gave warm encouragement to anxious, insecure students and to slow students.

It was encouraging to find that teachers related differently to students with different personality characteristics. The anxious, insecure student who is given close supervision and clear-cut structuring of activities probably feels more secure as the student is told exactly what is expected to be learned. Providing warm encouragement to anxious, insecure students or to slow students and clear intellectual challenges to self-assured or to bright students also seems to reflect good teaching practice. Since one of the goals of the individualized instruction program is to challenge bright students and to support and encourage slower students, it seems clear that the teachers who did so were following

Table 4. Projected Loadings of Teacher Reports of Treatment of Students (TRTS) in Student Personality Trait Space

Student Personality Factor	TRTS Scale	
	Eliciting-Permissive	Challenging
I. Group Involvement (Exvia)	.19	.02
II. Anxious Insecurity	-.55	-.66
III. Heedless Individual Gratification	-.54	.23
IV. Bright	.10	.42
Estimated Communality of Rating	.64	.67

Note: Adapted from Hummel-Rossi and Merrifield (1977).

the recommended teaching practices for individualized instruction programs. It is less clear why the teachers provided close supervision to assertive, tough-minded students. Perhaps in the freedom of the individualized instruction program, these students become too disruptive, or they do not progress in their lessons unless closely supervised. The teachers may also be keeping these students in their place, as it were, since teachers have been shown to reject assertive, active students (Feshbach, 1969; Helton, 1972).

Summary of the Students as Eighth Graders

Several important findings emerged from the investigation of these 219 students as eighth graders. Over the past fifteen years, the study of sex differences in student achievement has been a frequent topic of research and discussion. However, in the study reported here, correlations between sex and achievement as assessed by the SAT and by teacher-assigned grades were never greater than .24. Perhaps sex differences in achievement have in large part been environmentally and culturally determined, and they are gradually diminishing. It is also possible that the individualized instruction environment tends to reduce sex-role stereotyping by emphasizing each individual's growth independent of classmates.

The strengths of Figure Analogies and Word Grouping predictors of SAT scores related to four major subject areas provides clear support for the practical applicability of the TETRA model. The process of analyzing the curricula of the individualized instruction program and selecting tests called for by the model was clearly successful. Certainly, if the lengthy intelligence or aptitude batteries currently used in many junior high schools could be replaced by a few short, carefully selected aptitude tests, the counseling process would be greatly enhanced.

That there are different kinds of achievement criteria was shown, first, by the greater importance of aptitudes for the prediction of SAT scores and their lesser importance for the prediction of teacher-assigned grades and, second, by the significance of the TRTS measure for the prediction of teacher-assigned grades. Such achievement criteria as standardized achievement tests reflect a student's abilities to perform paper-and-pencil cognitive tasks within time limits and under structured conditions, while other criteria, like teacher-assigned grades, reflect a complex interpersonal interaction that develops over time and that is an indication of the student's ability to relate to a supervisor. One can argue for the need for both types of achievement evaluation. Unfortunately, the current trend in many school districts is away from use of standardized tests, and teacher grades are assuming greater importance as evaluations of student achievement. In schools that use individualized instruction programs in which each student progresses at his own rate, teacher-assigned grades may be the only indication of students' progress. However, our study raises some serious questions about the composition of this grade.

Finally, a troubling problem remains. When the relations between teacher treatment of student and student personality characteristics were examined, it was found that teachers responded differently toward individual students in a manner appropriate to the individual students' psychological needs. It appeared that teachers related to students in ways consistent with the recommended practices for individualized instruction. However, it was also found that student achievement was related to how the teacher perceived the student. A complex interaction may be occurring in which the teacher responds in an appropriate fashion to all students yet fosters greater achievement in some students than in others by this behavior.

The Students as Tenth Graders

In the follow-up study of these students two years later, it was not possible to obtain complete data on fifty-two students, who represented 24 percent of the sample. Some students were no longer attending the school, and some students did not have complete grade data because of class scheduling. It was decided not to compromise the data by estimating missing values. Therefore, at the risk of some selection bias, students with missing data were eliminated. The means for the remaining 167 students are presented in Table 5. Comparisons of means for the 167 students with means for the original sample of 219

Table 5. Prediction of Tenth Grade Teacher-Assigned Grades from SAT, Aptitudes, Sex, and Personality Traits

Eighth Grade Measures	Mean	S.D.	Correlations with Grade 10 Grades[a]							
			Zero Order				Increments to R^2			
			L[b]	M	S	SS	L	M	S	SS
SAT Reading Comprehension	109.70[c]	19.13	.40	.13	.24	.36	.01	.01	.00	.01
SAT Math Computations	101.68	22.68	.55	.38	.38	.49	.31*	.14*	.14*	.24*
SAT Math Concepts	102.41	15.75	.49	.40	.38	.46		.01		
SAT Math Applications	106.32	21.75	.49	.45	.43	.45		.10*	.02*	
SAT Spelling	100.66	24.33	.49	.20	.24	.35	.01			
SAT Language Use	108.22	24.32	.55	.25	.30	.44	.04*			
SAT Social Science	104.89	16.74	.47	.21	.38	.47				.03*
SAT Science	107.86	19.15	.41	.23	.42	.41			.08*	
Identical Pictures	63.48	13.26	.20	.01	.19	.14			.01	
Word Relations	10.89	3.65	.39	.31	.22	.34		.03*		
Symbol Manipulation	23.58	4.83	.21	.33	.23	.21	.01	.02*		
Omelet Test	18.18	5.20	.31	.06	.09	.20		.02*	.01	
Figure Analogies	17.31	5.60	.39	.35	.36	.36			.01	
Sign Changes	18.02	2.43	.44	.37	.28	.37		.01		
Gestalt Completion	29.96	6.23	.10	.00	.03	.00			.02*	.03*
Circle Reasoning	7.13	2.98	.37	.27	.27	.29	.03*			
Word Recognition	26.20	3.58	.20	.15	.10	.22				.02*
Bright	7.00[d]	1.72	.39	.27	.26	.40				.03*
Group Involvement[e]	1.92	5.48	.06	-.05	.06	-.05				.02*
Anxious Insecurity[e]	-.16	6.42	-.11	-.09	-.21	-.14			.01	.02*
Heedless Gratification[e]	-1.04	4.57	-.09	.04	.06	.01			.01	
Sex (Boy = 0, Girl = 1)	.47	.50	.00	-.16	-.13	.03	.00	.02*	.00	.00
Word Grouping	39.83	13.24	.32	.15	.20	.26				
TRTS - EP[f]	1.08	6.29	.63	.36	.47	.60				
TRTS - CH[f]	9.03	2.24	.33	.21	.31	.31				

Multiple R^2 = .41 .37 .32 .40

"Shrunken" Multiple R^2 = .39 .33 .27 .37

Note: N = 167; all values rounded to nearest hundreth.

[a]For zero-order correlations $p < .01$ for $|r| > .20$. For increments to R^2, significant predictors, $p < .05$, denoted by *. Only previously selected predictors used in analyses.

[b]L denotes Language Grades; M, Mathematics Grades; S, Science Grades; and SS, Social Studies Grades. All grades are from tenth grade teachers.

[c]All SAT values are grade equivalents; both means and standard deviations were multiplied by 10.

[d]Mean and standard deviation are from raw scores. Sten score corresponding to mean value = 6.

[e]Represents factor; high score indicated by name.

[f]Teacher ratings. EP, eliciting-permissive; CH, intellectually challenging; high scores indicated by name.

students (Table 2) show that the 167 students were probably a little stronger in aptitudes and achievement and were treated by their teachers in slightly more Eliciting-Permissive and Challenging manners.

To determine the degree to which tenth-grade teacher-assigned grades were dependent upon eighth-grade performance, tenth-year grades in language, mathematics, science, and social studies were predicted from eighth-grade SAT, aptitude, personality, and sex measures. Before the regression analyses were run, correlations were computed among all the predictors and criteria measures. With the aim of keeping the ratio between number of predictors and sample size as small as possible, the correlations were studied, and a few predictors were chosen. Separate predictors were chosen for each subject-area analysis. All possible SAT and aptitude measures were considered, as it was expected that aptitude-achievement relations in tenth grade would differ from aptitude-achievement relations in eighth grade. A hierarchical stepwise regression analysis was run for each subject area. First, the SAT Reading Comprehension and Math Computation subtests were forced into each equation to represent the prior achievement core. Next, remaining selected SAT subtests were entered. As in the eighth-grade analysis, the corresponding SAT subject-area subtest was used for each subject area, as well as the Spelling subtest for language grades and the Mathematics Applications subtest for mathematics and science grades. Then, selected aptitudes and personality traits were allowed to enter in a stepwise fashion. Finally, sex was entered. Results are presented in Table 5.

The findings are remarkably strong, given the time lapse and the nature of the criterion measures. The selected predictors accounted for 41 percent of the criterion variance in language grades, 37 percent in mathematics grades, 32 percent in science grades, and 40 percent in social studies grades. As the first predictor set, SAT Math Computation and one or two other SAT subtests accounted for at least 24 percent of the variance in tenth-year grades in each subject area. Comparison of correlations between corresponding subject area SAT scores and grades reveals a fairly small decrease from eighth to tenth grade. Considering next the aptitudes, Figure Analogies continues to show a strong relation to mathematics and science grades and a stronger relation to language and social studies grades in tenth grade than in eighth. Correlations from Circle Reasoning were about the same from eighth to tenth grade, while several of the correlations for Word Grouping decreased. For the other aptitudes considered, 3 percent was added for language grades, 7 percent for mathematics grades, 2 percent for science grades, and 5 percent for social studies grades. Of course, had SAT scores not been forced in as the first predictors, aptitudes would have accounted for considerably more of the variation in grades.

Bright maintained its correlations from eighth to tenth grade and contributed significantly to the prediction of social studies grades, as did Anxious

Insecurity and Heedless Individual Gratification. Sex was a significant predictor of mathematics grades, with boys doing better than girls; however, the relation was not strong ($r = -.16$).

In summary, concerning the stability of relations of aptitudes to performance, Figure Analogies and Circle Reasoning showed fairly consistent patterns from eighth to tenth grade in the prediction of teacher-assigned grades. Both these tests involve, according to the TETRA model, generating solutions to problems; in addition, Figure Analogies also involves evaluation of solutions and Circle Reasoning, transformation of solutions. Perhaps these aptitudes are fairly stable and important predictors of academic performance. The SAT subtests as indices of prior achievement showed good stability and were particularly strong in the corresponding subject areas. The low correlations between grades and personality traits were similar to the eighth-grade findings and call into question the utility of including personality tests in group testing programs—a common practice. Again, sex was found to have no important relation to achievement as defined by grades.

The reader will notice some rather striking correlations at the bottom of Table 5. The eighth-grade teachers' reports of how they treated their students showed fairly strong relations to students' tenth-grade achievement. Note that the correlations of Eliciting-Permissive with tenth-year language and social studies grades are .63 and .60, respectively. This implies that students who were treated in a permissive manner as eighth graders received higher grades from their tenth-grade teachers than students who were treated in a directing and monitoring manner as eighth graders.

To further investigate these relations, the sample of 167 students was first dichotomized for the Eliciting-Permissive measure and then for the Challenging measure. Points of dichotomy were chosen with consideration of the mean, median, and saddle points in the frequency distributions. Resulting group sizes were: high Eliciting-Permissive (EP, N = 97), low Eliciting-Permissive or Directive-Monitoring (DM, N = 70), high Challenging (CH, N = 104), and low Challenging or Warmly Encouraging (WE, N = 63). The correlation between Eliciting-Permissive and Challenging was roughly .25, about what it had been in the entire eighth-grade sample ($r = .29$).

Again, a hierarchical, stepwise regression solution was used. In all, twenty regression analyses were run: For each of the four subject areas, five groups were analyzed (the total sample and groups EP, DM, CH, and WE). As in the preceding analyses on tenth-grade students, the criteria were tenth-grade teacher-assigned grades in the four subject areas. SAT reading comprehension and mathematics computation were assigned the highest priority, then all sixteen aptitudes, Bright, the three personality components, and finally sex. The twenty tables of results are rather lengthy. For this reason, results have been summarized in Table 6. The interested researcher may obtain a complete copy of the twenty tables from the author.

Examining these results, one finds that eighth graders who have been

Table 6. Prediction of Tenth-Grade Teacher-Assigned Grades in Four Teacher Treatment Groups

Criterion: Tenth Grade Subject Area Teacher Grades	Group[b]	Sources of Predicted Variance (Increments to R^2)[a]				
		Tot	SAT	Apt	Per	Sex
Language	EP	43	40	03	-	-
	DM	56	24	26	04	02
	CH	43	34	08	-	01
	WE	52	42	09	01	-
Math	EP	53	32	21	-	-
	DM	40	19	18	-	03
	CH	36	20	10	04	02
	WE	65	39	26	-	-
Science	EP	51	39	11	01	-
	DM	35	15	15	05	-
	CH	43	32	09	-	02
	WE	36	16	10	10	-
Social Studies	EP	43	38	05	-	-
	DM	56	14	25	16	01
	CH	36	24	04	08	-
	WE	55	32	19	04	-

Note: N = 167, all values rounded to nearest hundredth and decimals omitted; the 20 tables from which these data are summarized are available from the author.

[a]Sources measured during eighth grade. SAT, Stanford Achievement Test subtests; Apt, aptitude tests; Per, Personality traits. Values are proportions of variance.
[b]Treatment groups. Ratings by eighth-grade teachers. EP, eliciting-permissive; DM, directive-monitoring; CH, intellectually challenging; WE, warmly encouraging.

directed and monitored, show later performance in social studies and language that is more predictable, 56 percent of the variance being accounted for in each, than the performance of students who were treated in an Eliciting-Permissive manner, 43 percent of the variance being accounted for in each. In both these subject areas, prior knowledge was the best predictor for students who had been treated in an Eliciting-Permissive manner, while aptitudes were better predictors for the group who had been directed and monitored. For the DM group in social studies, Word Arrangement, a test of semantic transformations, and Word Recognition, a test of semantic memory, were important, with each accounting for about 6 percent of the variance. Word Arrangement was also important for the DM group in language, accounting for 11 percent of the variance. Circle Reasoning accounted for an additional 5 percent in this group. For these two subject areas, personality traits did not seem to matter for the EP group, but they were important for the DM group. Group involvement alone accounted for 16 percent of the variance in the DM social studies group, with the less-involved students getting higher grades.

In contrast, the best overall predictions in mathematics and general science came from the EP group. Eighth-grade knowledge was again the better predictor, and again it was better for the EP group than for the DM group. However, in further contrast, the prediction from the aptitude measures was about the same for both groups in mathematics, but much greater (relative to R^2) in science. Aptitudes requiring symbolic and figural transformations were important for mathematics for both the EP and the DM groups, and aptitudes requiring spatial closure and transformations were important for science in the EP group, while two semantic tests, one requiring transformations (Word Arrangement) and the other convergent recall (Food Naming), were important to the DM science group. Personality traits made smaller contributions to the prediction of individual differences.

When one compares the effects of presenting a clear intellectual challenge to students with the effects of presenting warm encouragement and support, it is apparent that students who were given warm encouragement as eighth graders have more predictable grades as tenth graders in language, mathematics, and social studies but not in general science. Also, in language and mathematics, prior knowledge (SAT) is a better predictor for the WE group. For mathematics and social studies, aptitudes are stronger predictors in the WE group, with Figure Analogies accounting for 6 percent in the CH mathematics group and nine different aptitudes making significant contributions in the WE mathematics group. The Omelet Test alone accounted for 8 percent of the variance, and Symbol Manipulation, a symbolic coding test, accounted for 4 percent. This last aptitude test was also the strongest aptitude contributor (7 percent) for the WE social studies group. The next strongest was Word Recognition, a memory test for words presented without context (5 percent).

The relations of personality traits to performance were mixed: The self-centered student did better in the encouraged group in science, while the more socialized student did better in the challenged group in social studies.

In summary, with respect to the Eliciting-Permissive variable, it would seem that the more structured learning environment leads students who have special abilities to mobilize them to a greater degree for subsequent tasks. If it is true that students with weak skills will have somewhat inferior performance regardless of setting, it may follow that even high-aptitude students who have been treated permissively and who have come to expect their responses to be elicited will be less likely to be able to focus their talents on tasks assigned and to structure such tasks for themselves. After all, the organization of subject matter is the result of much intellectual input over a period of many years, and it is not, in general, easy to intuit. Considering the Challenge variable, it may be that challenge is inhibiting to some students, while encouragement inspires all students to do their best. All in all, it seems that a treatment combining direction, monitoring, and encouragement is more likely to facilitate learning. Clearly, these results point to the need for aptitude-treatment interaction studies in each of the subject areas studied so as to determine which treatment is most effective for the students who are high and the students who are low on the aptitudes identified with achievement.

Summary of the Students as Tenth Graders

Several important findings emerged from the follow-up study. As in the eighth-grade study, sex was not an important determinant of achievement. In language, where girls typically excel, there were no differences, and in mathematics, where boys usually excel, the typical superiority of boys was only very weakly supported. Results of this investigation, therefore, provide strong support for a cultural and environmental explanation of observed sex differences in school achievement.

Among the aptitude measures, the strong relation of Figure Analogies and Circle Reasoning to tenth-year grades as well as to eighth-year grades and the SAT scores suggests that the generation-of-solutions thought process, together with the subsequent evaluation- or transformation-of-solutions thought processes are important and stable determinants of achievement. Certainly, these tests warrant investigation in other settings as predictors of achievement. The good predictions provided by the SAT subscales both to tenth-year grades and to eighth-year grades supports the use of these subtests both as criteria for current achievement and as predictors of future achievement.

The finding that the eighth grade teachers' reports of how they treated their students were more important than aptitudes in predicting tenth-year grades was rather dramatic. For both eighth and tenth grades, students who were treated in an eliciting and permissive manner by their eighth-grade teachers received higher grades. The separate predictions conducted on students who were high and students who were low on the two TRTS measures clearly showed that aptitudes play the more important role when students are directed, monitored, and encouraged in their school work than when they are given freedom and clear intellectual challenges.

Comments and Suggestions

Aptitudes. The school administrator involved in planning a testing program should consider the Figure Analogies, Circle Reasoning, and Word Grouping aptitude tests as possible substitutes for more lengthy intelligence tests. Requiring a total testing time of less than twenty-five minutes, these three aptitude tests showed fairly strong relations with the achievement criteria, and they may provide predictions at least as good as many of the longer tests. If they are used in combination with a good measure of prior achievement, such as the SAT, more than adequate prediction of achievement can be obtained. Little support for the common practice of including personality tests has been found here, as the relation between personality traits and achievement proved quite weak. Further, as the group personality tests that are commonly used in the schools are not designed to identify serious adjustment or personality problems, they serve little use.

The need for a series of well-conceived aptitude treatment interaction (ATI) studies that build on the results of the investigation reported here is clearly indicated. If these results are examined in the context of the ATI literature, several observations can be made.

First, the results of ATI studies are often not significant, or if they are significant, they are not meaningful, because global ability measures were used. Analysis of curriculum for necessary aptitudes and selection of highly specific aptitude tests, as in this investigation, holds promise of accounting for more of the variation in measures of learning outcomes. This is especially true when the tests selected have good reliability and construct validity.

Second, many ATI studies are not well grounded in theory, and consequently they lead nowhere, except to another publication that will appear in a scholar's vita. When a theoretical model is used, it provides the foundation for building from one study to another. Without a theoretical model, it is difficult to tie the findings of separate studies together. The McDonald (1976) model of variables that influence teacher performance and children's learning of the Centra and Potter (1980) model of school and teacher variables that influence student learning could provide an appropriate framework for researchers in ATI. These models also provide a context in which several researchers, working together, could explore the dimensions of a single problem. This approach has particular merit for dissertation students who often lack experience in research and who could benefit immensely by interaction with their peers.

Third, it seems that many researchers who pursue ATI research judge it necessary to develop a somewhat artificial treatment and to manipulate it in an experimental setting. This leads to tight experimental control, which is not to be denigrated. However, as this investigation has shown, it is not necessary to develop such treatments. Many "treatments" exist and are implemented informally by teachers. Further, we have incomplete knowledge of these treatments. It seems preferable first to discover what these teacher treatments are and how they influence student learning and only then to experiment with new treatments. The TRTS measure evolved as a result of such thinking. We must spend more time in the classroom observing and analyzing the relation between what is happening and student learning.

Fourth, age is a variable that needs to be studied more thoroughly in ATI studies. Although age is usually given brief mention in the sample description, it is infrequently studied as an important variable in ATI studies. This is also true for studies of teacher expectations and teacher-student interaction. Yet age is a significant variable. A child's age is related to the child's receptivity to different types of instruction and to the development and differentiation of aptitudes, among other factors. For example, in his study of teaching effectiveness McDonald (1976) showed that teaching practices which were effective in second grade differed from teaching practices that were effective in fourth grade.

Fifth, consistent with the concern with age for the individual difference cross-sectional study, there is great need for researchers to stay with a population and to replicate findings at different ages, that is, to conduct longitudinal studies. It is only through such procedures that we can speak with some authority about stability of findings and developmental changes. A well-integrated ATI research program should provide for this aspect of growth in achievement.

The Teacher Report of Treatment of Students (TRTS) Measure. The TRTS measure was an experimental measure used for the first time in this investigation. It appears to have tapped an important teacher-reported behavior related to student achievement. However, before the measure is used again, its validity and reliability need further investigation; some recommendations follow. A researcher who pursues this area of study should first investigate reliability and validity in a setting and with a population similar to those encountered in this investigation and then move on to other settings and populations.

First, to examine validity, the relation between how the teacher reports treating students and how the teacher actually treats students needs to be investigated through an observational study. For the purposes of this study, an observational rating scale must be developed to assess overt manifestations of the Eliciting-Permissive and Challenging constructs. Teachers should be observed on a number of occasions in different individualized instruction teaching situations in junior high school. These observational reports should then be summarized and examined against each of teacher's reports. To be most effective, this procedure should be carried out at least three times (for example, in October, February, and May) during a single school year. Researchers should be aware that teachers' behavior can change during the school year. Finally, children should be interviewed at the same times and asked how their teachers treated them. These findings should be related to the teachers' reports.

Second, the stability of the measure should be investigated by repeated measurements of the same set of teachers on the same students. Each child should be assessed by at least three teachers. Four questions need to be asked: Are within-teacher measures stable across occasions? Are between-teacher measures consistent across occasions? Is there a relation between teacher treatment of students and the teacher's subject area, and if there is, what are these relations? Are students with certain aptitudes or personality traits rated with greater reliability, validity, or both? If so, what are these aptitudes or traits? Research by Brophy and others (1975) and a review of measures of teaching behavior by Shavelson and Dempsey-Atwood (1976) indicated that global measures are the most stable teacher behavior measures. The stability of the TRTS, which is a global albeit two-dimensional measure, should be put in the context of these authors' findings after the studies just described have been completed.

Third, the TRTS was used in a junior high school individualized instruction setting. After the validity and reliability of the TRTS have been investigated in a similar setting and the necessary changes have been made, the measure should be studied in other instructional formats (for example, in lectures and in small-group discussions) and across other grades. This will require repeating studies parallel to those outlined for the junior high school in which individualized instruction is emphasized. Readers should consider that there may be a relation between teacher aptitudes, expectations for students, and teacher treatment of students. Assessing teachers will be difficult, but McDonald's (1976) work in this area should provide direction.

Finally, do not become overly attached to the TRTS. Think about the constructs assessed by the scale. Perhaps a new scale should be developed. This brings us to consider the construct of controlling student learning.

Control. The dimension of control or direction emerged as an important teacher variable related to student achievement. Although their methodologies, sample characteristics, and construct operationalization differed from those used for this investigation, Soar (1972) and Evertson and Brophy (1973) found positive relations between teacher control and student gains in achievement on standardized tests, and Cooper, Hinkel, and Good (1980) found a positive relation between teacher expectations and teacher perceptions of control over student performance. The concept of teacher control or direction of students may be extremely important to student achievement, and it needs to be investigated thoroughly as it relates to student aptitude and achievement. First, more attention needs to be paid to operationalization of the concept and to development of an adequate measurement instrument. Second, as results from this investigation point to interaction with aptitudes, control should be studied in an ATI framework. Providing partial support for this opinion, Brophy (1979, p. 744) noted: "A great many important but yet undiscovered determinants of student learning will be found by studying such variables as the kinds of assignments teachers make, the ways these assignments are presented and explained, and the methods teachers use to monitor performance on the assignments and provide correction."

If we really want to know why Jimmy is learning mathematics easily and Johnny is having great difficulty, we, as researchers, must dig our heels in and address ourselves to the tough theoretical and measurement questions through systematic ATI interaction studies. As Cronbach and Snow (1977, p. 521) advised, we should make the "development of aptitude a goal of instruction." This is a difficult charge but one that we are capable of meeting, if we try.

References

Barnard, J., Zimbardo, P., and Sarason, S. "Teachers' Ratings of Student Personality Traits as They Relate to IQ and Social Desirability." *Journal of Educational Psychology,* 1968, *59,* 128–132.

Bennett, G. K., Seashore, H. G., and Wesman, A. G. *Fifth Edition Manual for the Differential Aptitude Tests, Form S and T.* New York: Psychological Corporation, 1974.

Braun, C. "Teacher Expectation: Sociopsychological Dynamics." *Review of Educational Research,* 1976, *46,* 185–213.

Brophy, J. E. "Teacher Behavior and Its Effects." *Journal of Educational Psychology,* 1979, *71,* 733–750.

Brophy, J. E., Coulter, C. L., Crawford, W. J., Evertson, C. M., and King, C. E. "Classroom Observational Scales: Stability Across Time and Context and Relationships with Student Learning Gains." *Journal of Educational Psychology,* 1975, *67,* 873–881.

Brophy, J., and Good, T. "Teachers' Communication of Differential Expectations for Children's Classroom Performance: Some Behavioral Data." *Journal of Educational Psychology,* 1970, *61,* 365–374.

Cattell, R. B. "Theory of Fluid and Crystallized Intelligence: A Critical Experiment." *Journal of Educational Psychology,* 1963, *54,* 1–22.

Cattell, R. B. *The Scientific Analysis of Personality.* New York: Penguin Books, 1965.

Cattell, R. B. *Junior-Senior High School Personality Questionnaire.* Champaign, Ill.: Institute for Personality and Ability Testing, 1968.

Cattell, R. B., and Cattell, M. D. L. *Handbook for the Junior-Senior High School Personality Questionnaire.* Champaign, Ill.: Institute for Personality and Ability Testing, 1969.

Cattell, R. B. *Abilities: Their Structure, Growth, and Action.* Boston: Houghton Mifflin, 1971a.

Cattell, R. B. *Handbook of Modern Personality Theory.* Chicago: Aldine, 1971b.

Centra, J. A., and Potter, D. A. "School and Teacher Effects: An Interrelational Model." *Review of Educational Research,* 1980, *50,* 273–291.

Cooper, H., Hinkel, G., and Good, T. "Teachers' Beliefs About Interaction Control and Their Observed Behavioral Correlates." *Journal of Educational Psychology,* 1980, *72,* 345–354.

Cronbach, L., and Snow, R. *Aptitudes and Instructional Methods: A Handbook for Research on Interactions.* New York: Irvington, 1977.

d'Heurle, A., Mellinger, J. C., and Haggard, E. A. "Personality, Intellectual, and Achievement Patterns in Gifted Children." *Psychological Monographs,* 1959, *73* (entire issue).

Dermen, D., French, J. W., and Harman, H. H. *Guide to Factor-Referenced Temperament Scales.* Princeton, N.J.: Educational Testing Service, 1978.

Ekstrom, R. B. *Cognitive Factors: Some Recent Literature.* Technical Report 2. Princeton, N.J.: Educational Testing Service, 1973.

Ekstrom, R. B., French, J. W., and Harman, H. H. *Kit of Factor-Referenced Cognitive Tests.* Princeton, N.J.: Educational Testing Service, 1976.

Elmore, P. B., and Vasu, E. L. "Relationship Between Selected Variables and Statistics Achievement: Building a Theoretical Model." *Journal of Educational Psychology,* 1980, *72,* 457–467.

Evertson, C. M., and Brophy, J. E. *High-Inferenced Behavioral Ratings as Correlates of Teaching Effectiveness.* Austin: Research and Development Center for Teacher Education, University of Texas, 1973.

Feshbach, N. D. "Student Teacher Preferences for Elementary School Pupils Varying in Personality Characteristics." *Journal of Educational Psychology,* 1969, *60,* 126–132.

French, J. W. *Toward the Establishment of Self-Report Temperament Factors Through Literature Search and Interpretation.* Princeton, N.J.: Educational Testing Service, 1973. (ERIC document ED 080 579.)

Gardner, E. F., Mervin, J. C., Callis, R., and Madden, R. *Stanford Achievement Test: High School Basic Battery.* New York: Harcourt Brace Jovanovich, 1965.

Gebhart, G. G., and Hoyt, D. P. "Personality Needs of Under- and Over-Achieving Freshmen." *Journal of Applied Psychology,* 1958, *42,* 125–128.

Good, T., and Grouws, D. *Reaction of Male and Female Teacher Trainees to Descriptions of Elementary School Pupils.* Technical Report No. 62. Columbia: Center for Research in Social Behavior, University of Missouri, 1972.

Hakstian, A. R., and Cattell, R. B. "Examination of Adolescent Sex Differences in Some Ability and Personality Traits." *Canadian Journal of Behavioral Sciences,* 1975, *7,* 295–312.

Helton, G. "Teacher Attitudinal Response to Selected Characteristics of Elementary School Students." Unpublished doctoral dissertation, University of Texas at Austin, 1972.

Hummel-Rossi, B., and Merrifield, P. "Student Personality Factors Related to Teacher Reports of Their Interactions with Students." *Journal of Educational Psychology,* 1977, *69,* 375–380.

Jeter, J., and Davis, O. "Elementary School Teachers' Differential Classroom Interaction with Children as a Function of Differential Expectations of Pupil Achievements." Paper presented at the annual meeting of the American Educational Research Association, New Orleans, March 1973.

Krug, R. E. "Over- and Underachievement and the Edwards Personal Preference Schedule." *Journal of Applied Psychology,* 1959, *43,* 133–136.

McDonald, F. J. *Beginning Teacher Evaluation Study: Phase II, 1973–74 — Summary Report.* Princeton, N.J.: Educational Testing Service, 1976.

Merrifield, P., and Hummel-Rossi, B. "Redundancy in the Stanford Achievement Test." *Educational and Psychological Measurement,* 1976, *36,* 997–1001.

Merrill, R. M., and Murphy, D. T. "Personality Factors and Academic Achievement in College." *Journal of Counseling Psychology,* 1959, *6,* 207–210.

Nason, L. J. *Academic Achievement of Gifted High School Students.* Los Angeles: University of Southern California Press, 1958.

Shavelson, R., and Dempsey-Atwood, N. K. "Generalizability of Measures of Teaching Behavior." *Review of Educational Research,* 1976, *46,* 533–611.

Snow, R. E. "Research on Aptitude for Learning: A Progress Report." In L. S. Shulman (Ed.), *Review of Research in Education.* Vol. 4. Itasca, Ill.: Peacock, 1976.

Soar, R. S. *Follow Through Classroom Process Measurement and Pupil Growth.* Gainesville: Institute for Development of Human Resources, College of Education, University of Florida, 1972.

Wechsler, D. *Manual for the Wechsler Intelligence Scale for Children, Revised.* New York: Psychological Corporation, 1974.

Willis, S. "Formation of Teachers' Expectations of Students' Academic Performance." Unpublished doctoral dissertation, University of Texas at Austin, 1972.

Barbara Hummel-Rossi is associate professor and director, Program in Evaluation and Measurement, Department of Educational Psychology, New York University.

A model of thinking based on four processes and four contents of thought is proposed. Similarities to and differences from Guilford's structure of intellect are noted. Implications for school-related testing are discussed.

A Tetrahedral Model of Intelligence

Philip Merrifield

Recorded history is full of references to intelligence and to differences of intelligence between people. The choices made by Ulysses on his travels, Gideon's solution to his personnel selection problem, and the relating of physique to cognitive style exemplified by Caesar's comment on Cassius are but a few instances from older times. It is interesting to note that, although personality traits have long been seen as diverse, intellectual capacity has traditionally been seen as unitary. In the philosophy and nascent psychology of the eighteenth century, faculty psychology was an exception, but it failed to attract many adherents because of undue fractionation and overextension (for example, the Spurzheim promotion of phrenology) due in large part from lack of convincing empirical evidence. More recently, the interpretation of the work of Binet as measuring a single quantity and its mathematization by Stern into the intelligence quotient was eagerly adopted by those responsible for mass education. It seemed to them that such a quotient, alleged to have an amazing amount of stability over time and notable resistance to training, would be very useful in sorting out children and adults for placement in various kinds of training programs. Unfortunately, schooling became "school," and the narrowing focus of learning to include primarily language-related achievements, with a modicum of numerical skills, led to a shift from different kinds of training to different levels of one kind of training and thus to the more insidious forms of tracking.

P. Merrifield (Ed.). *New Directions for Testing and Measurement: Measuring Human Abilities,* no. 12.
San Francisco: Jossey-Bass, December 1981.

A second unfortunate result of the emphasis on a monolithic view of intelligence is the implication that only one kind of processing of information can be considered respectable. Again, the "school" emphasis has increased the focus on memory and on a limited form of evaluation, with much less emphasis on generative or productive processing and almost none on transformational thinking, except in language-related, school achievement oriented tasks.

The Problem

The needs of the establishment — not only "school" but the broader society it was intended to serve — to measure and compare students with regard to their achievements have been persistent; education has been seen, correctly, as a means of social and financial advancement (assuming that higher income, more material goods, and greater envy from one's associates are measures of an advanced state of existence, if not of grace). The response of psychometrists to these needs has been to develop extensive systems of tests and to accumulate great masses of data on relative performance in many subject matter areas. It happened that language skills and number skills were easier to measure reliably and that the processes of thinking which could be most easily described quantitatively were related to memory and evaluation. Thus, through the best of intentions, a major problem was redefined into a more restricted one for which a reasonably efficient solution seemed rapidly obtainable.

The major problem, however, remains: the quantification of processes other than memory, for contents or modes of expression not easily expressed in language or in simple numerical terms. While it is clear that persons do differ in capability to learn language and related skills, and thus to learn about the world in terms of verbal labels and verbally stated relations, other modes of abilities should be applied to the task of learning and to the need to cope. For many experiences, language is not the most direct channel for transmitting or acquiring information, although we as a species have been exceedingly clever in using language to make do in many domains. The differences in the colors and odors of a rose and a marigold are exceedingly difficult to describe in language, as are the timbre of a singer's voice, or the composition of a statue, or the warmth of a lover's hand.

The requirements for defining intelligence in terms of several different kinds of processing and several different kinds of content may be sufficient for describing the state of the thinker or the learner. But in the presence of material to be learned, a third component must be considered: the ability to address material at differing levels of complexity. Should one attend to just the meaning of a word, or consider it as part of sentence, or as a set of letters? Is a paragraph to be understood as a single idea, or as a system of words related to each other by sequence and syntax? Is a portrait only a means of identification, or should we attend to the painter's choice of palette, style, and detail to represent his view of the character of the subject? The glib answer to such disjunctive questions is, of course, "yes!" A moment's reflection brings the realization that that answer is also true. The critical issue, however, is not whether the material is labelled as simple or complex by the teacher or the expert but whether the learner can direct his attention to differing levels of complexity, depending upon his needs for information from the material at that time. All three of these concerns — processes, contents, and the role of attention — will be elaborated in subsequent sections.

The Tetra Model

Thurstone (1938, 1947) developed applications of factor analysis which led to the convincing empirical data for differential aptitudes that had not been available to earlier proponents of such a theory. His work was followed in the United States by J. P. Guilford and John Flanagan, to mention only two leaders; the extensive work of R. B. Cattell in England and in this country has led to a similar collection of descriptions of aptitudes. Cattell (1971) has preferred to describe these aptitudes as manifestations of fluid intelligence in various crystallized entities, while Guilford (1967) has, until recently, inclined more toward aptitudes as co-equal aspects of intelligence. Despite their differences, Cattell and Guilford agree on the description of some nineteen aptitudes for which reliable measures are available and appropriate for various age levels (Merrifield, 1975). These and other aptitude measures are described in the recent Kit of Factor-Referenced Cognitive Tests (Ekstrom and others, 1976).

Conceptual Considerations

In the TETRA model, there are four processes and four contents. An aptitude is defined as the application of a single process to a thought expressed in a single content. Using the gerundive form to highlight the dynamic nature of the processes, these are called *remembering, evaluating, generating,* and *transforming.* The content areas are called *self, forms, ideas,* and *persons.* These categories are broad, but there is little overlap. As aptitude is defined, there are 4 × 4 (or sixteen) basic aptitudes made up of the applications of the four processes to each of the four content areas. The processes and contents are elaborated later, but space does not permit fuller specification of the sixteen aptitudes.

It must be emphasized that most tasks of interest in school settings or those encountered in daily living involve the activation of more than one of the sixteen aptitudes. Thus, the model for learning (or for coping) is not the selection and exercise of a single aptitude in a situation, but rather the marshalling of a set of aptitudes in an appropriate array. Intelligent conduct is to be modeled by at least a regression equation with many predictors, if not a more complex multivariate representation. The informational needs that the intelligent person brings to a situation determine the appropriate level of complexity to be attended to; the same situation may be perceived as needing different levels of analysis or input at different times. Practice in attending to different levels of complexity can be provided in a structured way. The same material may be used repeatedly, if it is rich enough, with the learner's attention being directed at successive stages to levels of increasing complexity, or to greater consolidation and generalization, whichever the teacher considers more appropriate at that moment of learning. It may be no service to the learner for the teacher to break down complex entities into smaller pieces to be learned. Not only does this procedure often result in the perception that the pieces themselves are unrelated, but the process of integration and synthesis into meaningful wholes is deprived of a schema. Were the learner taught the technique of focusing attention on different levels of complexity of the initial whole, then as he takes it apart (actually or vicariously) the inherent structure would become more familiar and serve as a guide to the reconstruction of the whole.

At some risk, as we do not wish to enter the heredity-environment controversy here, we suggest that the sixteen basic aptitudes may be related to the potentials available to all humans and that the developed abilities and skills result in part from maturation and, in perhaps larger part, from appropriate direction of the learner's attention to the various levels of complexity of events in our experience.

The two tetrads for processes and contents are shown in Figure 1. We shall first discuss the processes of thought and then the contents in which the thoughts are expressed. The examples given are for illustration of only the salient process or content in a more-or-less familiar task or experience; as noted above, coping and learning typically require the concerted application of a set of several aptitudes, each of which is defined as the co-acting of one process on thoughts expressed in one content. While the tetrads could be oriented with any process or any content at the top, it seems reasonable to arrange them as we have, as *transforming* has some managerial overtones, and *self* has a certain centrality.

Processes

Remembering. The process of *remembering* involves the familiar recognition and recall, such as vocabulary in a language, number facts, spelling of names, dates, relations among persons, melodies, spatial locations, and pathways. Remembering also involves the strategies of storing information, as well as retrieving it, although the storage process might better be called "membering." In the TETRA model, remembering includes both short-term and long-term memory.

Evaluating. As described in this model, *evaluating* is more than just the selection of or convergence upon the right answer. It includes as well as the processes of making judgments in ambiguous situations, deciding on relevant

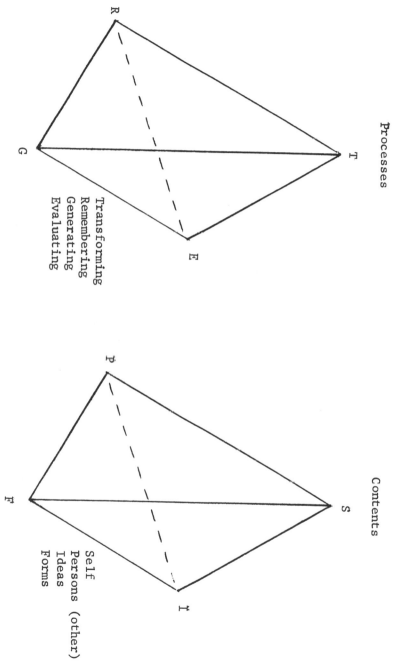

Figure 1. The Tetrahedral Model of Intelligence

Processes

Contents

Transforming
Remembering
Generating
Evaluating

Self
Persons (other)
Ideas
Forms

criteria, choosing amongst ambiguous alternatives, and placing a value on the goodness of fit of some given information to some given standard. The field of literary criticism is a complex instance of evaluating, and diction is a lesser example. Evaluation is involved in other activities: deciding that one representational system is more elegant in the sense of parsimony coupled with completeness; aesthetic considerations in general, in the visual arts, music, literature, or even in science; questions of provenance and authorship; interpretations of observed behaviors; and valuing, in terms of social cost and benefit, the utilities of various political actions.

Generating. This process is similar to an operation defined by Guilford (1967) as productive thinking; it is of historical interest that productive thinking as a category was prior to the more well-known divergent and convergent thinking in the SOI model. The distinction between divergent and convergent thinking has been overdrawn by popular writers, and by some psychologists so that the two operations have seemed to be opposites and even mutually exclusive. This is not the case. In the TETRA model, divergent thinking is the combination of remembering and generating, while the combination of generating and evaluating is convergent thinking. As examples of generating, it is salient in the development of plots and characters in a novel, in providing proofs in geometry, in cooking, in decoration, in planning a party, and in evolving an opinion of one's own self.

Transforming. Finally, the process that represents the greatest departure from the SOI model is *transforming.* Guilford considers transformations as one of the products, but it is much more active than that. In the TETRA model, transforming is the act of changing procedures, of reinterpreting situations, of reconstructing frameworks of associations within memory. Specific examples would include the double entendre, the juxtapositions that underlie much humor and satire, the current interest in revisionist biography and history, and even punning (or even odd punning). In music, transposition of key is a simple example of transforming, while a more complicated event is the presentation, as in *Kismet,* of a Borodin theme as a love song, or especially using the same theme both as a ballad and as a rousing march, as in *Music Man;* classical music, for example, Bach's fugues, provides prime examples of transformations of themes and figures. In art, the *trompe l'oeil* is an excellent example, as are Escher's works, and using the same basic form but different sizes, colors, and orientations.

In computer programming, the use of various transforming skills leads to more elegant programs and to greater flexibility in data processing. In the social arena, reinterpretations involved in salary negotiations are examples, as are modifications of various forms of therapy. The student's ability to adopt at will a different point of view and to accept — at least for a time — a different interpretation of the same event is another instance, one of obvious importance in education. The creative synthesis of a variety of approaches to works of art, to science experiments and phenomena, and to social situations all utilize the process of transforming, not only of the person's perceptions of the material but also of the organization of relevant associations in memory, the freeing up of what had been bound into a stereotype, and the reorganization into a new whole.

In Figure 2, the three sides of the process tetrahedron, with *transforming* at its apex are shown. I am greatly indebted to Serge Madhere (1980) for the conceptualizations presented in Figure 2, particularly those relating the steps in the TEG and the TER faces to Piaget's monumental work. The reader may wish to refer to Chapters 5 and 12 in Piaget's concise presentation of *Structuralism* (1970) for common ground shared by that work and the TETRA model.

The bottom face, not explicitly shown, defined by *remembering, evaluating,* and *generating,* seems to cover a great deal of what is usually emphasized in school achievement. Along the *remembering–evaluating* edge is what is called *cognition* in the SOI model; all material needed is in memory, which is probed by the evaluating process until a proper match is found to some given criteria. An example is a multiple-choice test of vocabulary. The criterion for the match may itself come from memory, or, as one may infer from the *evaluating–generating* edge, the learner may build search models and develop criteria to be used in cognition. As noted before, this edge represents the SOI operation of convergent thinking; Madhere (1980) suggests that it may also be called *scanning,* in Piagetian terms, as the learner constructs and/or modifies schemata to serve in the organization and storage of his or her experiences. It may be noted that this bottom face seems to be unrelated to *transforming.* Yet is there ever a time when that uniquely human process is not part of human life? Probably not. Transforming may have as its first function the awakening and development of the other processes so that the infant can begin to make sense of what, as James speculated, is "blooming, buzzing confusion." One should not view the process tetrahedron as static, but rather with transforming rising as the child matures.

The levels shown for the view of the sides of the tetrahedron in Figure 2 depict primarily semantic activities in SOI terms. Analogous presentations for the other SOI content categories have not been developed. At this writing, it is doubtful that the level-for-level correspondence which would be completely analogous to the SOI treatment of products will be necessary.

Contents

The four content areas in this model of intelligence (see Figure 1) deal with ideas, forms, other persons, and the self. As with the processes, the Guilford content categories can be seen as combinations of these domains. Three of his categories result from the outreaching of the *self* to the other three. The dynamic interaction of *self* to *ideas* leads to the SOI semantic category, or meanings typically, but not necessarily expressed in language; *self* to *forms* results in figural content, including the sensory inputs (Guilford has recently

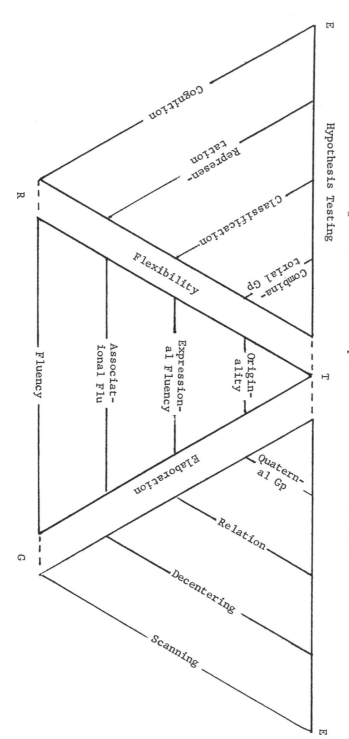

Figure 2. Further Development of the Process Tetrahedron

separated figural into visual and auditory); and, *self* to *persons* describes the realm of behavioral or social intelligence. Guilford's fourth content, *symbolic* — by which he means essentially arbitrary systems of signs or codes — arises in TETRA from the attribution of meanings to signs or the edge *ideas* to *forms.* It is interesting that his edge has no direct connection to *self;* perhaps those children who insist that they just "can't relate to math" are quite correct in their introspections. In discussing this tetrahedron of contents in which thoughts are expressed, let us begin with the most innovative, shown at the top of the tetrahedron.

Self. In the Guilford model, social intelligence was depicted as "behavioral" content; while it was initially intended to imply all human interpersonal activity, it shortly became focused on behavior of other persons, and how the thinker intellectualizes his or her perceptions of that behavior. In the TETRA model, self serves to help define the SOI categories of semantic, figural, and behavioral. Self, in TETRA, refers to the concept of one's own being, as one acts in everyday life. Treating self as an object of thought, or as a medium of expression, implies that we can bring our attention to bear on our own behavior and then apply the four processes to what is observed (Merrifield, 1971). We each can consider ourself as we interact with ideas, with forms, and with other persons; we can remember, evaluate, generate, and perhaps even transform those interactions. Perception of self, by itself, requires greater intellectual effort; at a foundational level, one can consider himself as he takes on various roles — a useful approach to the assessment of self-concept (Jordan and Merrifield, 1981).

Persons. This designates our perceptions of the behavior of other persons, particularly the various cues other than clearly stated intentions (for instance, stance, inflection of the voice, gesture, and facial expressions). A good deal of conventional wisdom (learned from elders informally) is involved here, making this category relatively culture bound, even though some body language is nearly universal. Behavior of persons in groups, from the bridge club to political parties and governments, are included here; procedures for differentiating persons from each other are also part of this broad domain.

It was noted above that the edge from *forms* to *ideas* corresponded to the symbolic category in the SOI; it is interesting that the edges from *persons* to *forms* and from *persons* to *ideas* are as yet unassociated; the reader may wish to speculate regarding those potentials.

Ideas. Ideas have long loomed large in the work of philosophers. In this model, the category includes concept (as a linguistic device), most names of things, connotations that are either culture-based or more intuitional, linguistic systems as they contribute to meanings, specific meanings of words, and the like. Language characterizes a large fraction of our interactions with other persons in our environment, as well as with ideas themselves. Ideas, in this model, is broader than language, however, and is to include all representations that clearly, that is, by cultural agreement, convey an established meaning to others (or, in the psychoanalytic context, to one's self). Traffic signs, religious symbols, the meanings of mathematical notations, and the like, are included in this domain of ideas or meanings.

Forms. This category is concerned with spatial configurations, tastes, odors, tactile impressions, kinesthetics, colors, sounds, and other sensory aspects of our environment. Most assessment in this domain has been made with visual forms, typically in black and white, but those measures have barely skimmed the surface of differentiated responses to forms of various sorts. Much experimental work has been aimed at establishing such differentiation, but those procedures have seldom found their way into psychometric application in group testing. Obviously, to learn more about this domain of human response, test makers must adapt to more laboratory-like procedures. Forms of various sorts have been widely used in the assessment of infant intelligence, where reliance on reliable language behavior is premature; because in our culture, these responses to forms are among the least often formally learned, they have been favored by those seeking measures of culture-fair measures of intelligence. It is, thus, of more than passing concern that such measures, based on responses to forms, as described more fully by Hennessy (this volume), are being seen increasingly as probably biased, precisely because the forms are unfamiliar to the respondents and more so to minority group members than to those who grow into the mainstream where toys and games are more common (Scheuneman, this volume).

Technical Comments

It is intended that the empirical evidence for the sixteen basic aptitudes will be factors as defined by Thurstone (1947). The requirement of full-count hyperplanes, each containing a measure representing each other factor, will be observed. Measures of these aptitudes will be considered adequate to the degree that they represent only one aptitude (are univocal). While linear independence of factors is the minimum requirement, orthogonality is more consistent with parsimony, and thus more greatly desired. A measure of an aptitude will be considered minimally adequate only if the reliable portion of its residual is substantial after it has been regressed on measures of other aptitudes. Ideally, the larger this portion the better, as is in keeping with the desire for univocality.

Guilford (1981) has accepted the possibility of second-order and higher-order factors in the SOI context, based on re-analysis of correlations from some of the later studies done under his supervision of the Aptitudes Research Project (Guilford, 1967). While the possibility that such analyses could be fruitful may derive from some falling short of the objectives of constructing tests to measure orthogonal factors in the SOI, it is also possible that the SOI factors are correlated because they share certain more basic aspects, such as the processes and contents described in TETRA. It is easy to draw the implication from Guilford's 1981 article that what were once labels of categories in the SOI are now to be considered as factors of intelligence, and to this position we must protest; a factor must depict an action and an action must have an object, a focus, a thing thought about.

Lest the reader think from our previous comments that we are living in the past, we shall comment also on a recent development in research on intelligence. Limitations of space force us to consider the work of only one leader in this new movement as an example. Whitely (1980, 1981) looks forward to the description of an aptitude test by a unidimensional latent trait model, a congenial idea to one familiar with Thurstone's (1947) accounting equation. It may be significant that neither Thurstone, Guilford, nor Cattell are cited in either of these two articles. In the latent trait method applied to components, aptitude test items are rewritten to focus on subtasks; scores on these tasks are then combined to predict the initial scores on the aptitude test. While this approach is interesting, it seems too quick to accept a test as equivalent to an aptitude, especially since most factorists recommend that factors be estimated as composites of several tests, if not as factor scores per se. The fractionation into components seems to involve unavoidable sequential dependencies, and thus the correlations among these scores are distorted; use of such correlations in regression, multiple regression or structural equations can lead to quite uninterpretable results. The regression of item scores on the newly defined components seems formally equivalent to the description of such scores by regressing them on factor scores as defined long ago (Thurstone, 1947).

Despite my negative comments, I believe we need to look more closely at the basic definitions of aptitudes as combinations of processes and contents and to seek diligently for empirical evidence of differential abilities, whether we finally call them factors or components or something else.

Summary

The TETRA model is a proposal for tetrahedra representing four processes and four contents. Examination of the process tetrahedron suggests that all of the SOI operations, plus others, can be described as combinations of the TETRA processes; further, Piagetian levels may also be described, with the chronologically later stages involving more of the process called Transforming than do the earlier stages. (Figures 1, 2)

The four contents (Figure 1) may be combined to define SOI content categories, plus others. *Semantic, figural,* and *behavioral* are seen as interactions of *self* with *ideas, forms* and *persons,* respectively.

Attention to level of complexity is seen to have an important role in learning, as the learner mobilizes an appropriate subset of the sixteen basic aptitudes (four processes crossed with four contents) to attack a problem. The appropriate complexity, however, is determined by the learner's experience and needs and is not an inherent aspect of the task, as is implied by the product category in the SOI.

Guilford's acceptance (1981) of higher-order factors is not too surprising since his operations and contents share the more basic processes and content areas of the TETRA model. Recent efforts to study intelligence through

98

the latent trait analysis of components is commendable but is seen as formally equivalent to the description of tests as predicted from factor scores. Workers in this area are encouraged to study the principles of test construction used in developing the extensive array of items developed under the guidance of factor theories of intelligence.

References

Cattell, R. B. *Abilities: Their Structure, Growth, and Action.* Boston: Houghton Mifflin, 1971.

Ekstrom, R. B., French, J. W., Harman, H. H., and Derman, D. "Manual for Kit of Factor-Referenced Cognitive Tests." Princeton, N.J.: Educational Testing Service, 1976.

Guilford, J. P. "Higher-Order Structure-of-Intellect Abilities." *Multivariate Behavioral Research,* 1981, *4* (16), 411–436.

Guilford, J. P. *Nature of Human Intelligence.* New York: McGraw-Hill, 1967.

Jordan, T. J., and Merrifield, P. R. "Self-Concepting: Another Aspect of Aptitude." In M. D. Lynch, A. A. Norem-Hebeisen, and K. J. Gergen (Eds.), *Self-Concept: Advances in Theory and Research.* Cambridge, Mass.: Ballinger, 1981.

Madhere, S. "Developmental Considerations on the Tetrahedron of Intellectual Processes." Unpublished manuscript, New York University, April 1980.

Merrifield, P. R. "Review of Cattell's Abilities: Their Structure, Growth, and Action." *American Educational Research Journal,* 1975, *4* (12), 515–521.

Merrifield, P. R. "Using Measured Intelligence Intelligently." In R. Cancro (Ed.), *Intelligence.* New York: Grune and Stratton, 1971.

Piaget, J. *Structuralism.* New York: Basic Books, 1970.

Thurstone, L. L. *Vectors of the Mind.* Chicago: University of Chicago Press, 1938.

Thurstone, L. L. *Multiple Factor Analysis.* Chicago: University of Chicago Press, 1947.

Whitely, S. E. "Latent Trait Models in the Study of Intelligence." *Intelligence,* 1980, *2* (4), 97–132.

Whitely, S. E. "Measuring Aptitude Processes with Multicomponent Latent Trait Models." *Journal of Educational Measurement,* 1981, *2* (18), 67–84.

Philip Merrifield is professor and director, Program in Psychoeducational Research, Measurement, and Evaluation, New York University.

Index